A Student's Guide to JEWISH AMERICAN Genealogy

Oryx American Family Tree Series

A Student's Guide to JEWISH AMERICAN Genealogy

By Jay Schleifer

Oryx Press
1996

To Rivkah

Copyright 1996 by The Rosen Publishing Group, Inc.
Published in 1996 by The Oryx Press
4041 North Central at Indian School Road
Phoenix, Arizona 85012-3397

Printed and bound in the United States of America

∞ The paper used in this publication meets the minimum
requirements of American National Standard for Information
Science—Permanence of Paper for Printed Library Materials,
ANSI Z39.48, 1984.

Schleifer, Jay.
    A student's guide to Jewish American genealogy / by Jay Schleifer.
        p.   cm. — (Oryx American family tree series)
    Includes bibliographical references and index.
    ISBN 0-89774-977-4
    1. Jewish Americans—Genealogy—Handbooks, manuals, etc.
    2. Jewish Americans—Genealogy—Bibliography.   I. Title.
    II. Series.
    E184.J5S33184   1996
    929'.1'089924073—dc20   96-937
                                                                       CIP
                                                                       AC

Contents

Chapter 8. Gaining Knowledge from Family Members, 114

Chapter 9. Searching for Records, 128

Chapter 10. Research on the Holocaust and Your Ancestors' Roots, 147

Chapter 1
The Box in the Closet

If you're reading this book, it could be because you've found the box in the closet.

Many Jewish homes have such a box. It's filled with old photos, greeting cards, and papers of many sizes but mostly one color—yellow, from age.

You recognize some of the contents of the box: There are pictures of you when you were younger, and of others in your family when *they* were younger. Your uncle is there too, leaning on the tailfin of a 1950s car and looking very different from the man you know today. Someone's high school diploma is in the box. So is a pressed flower from somebody's senior prom.

Other items, though, are harder to identify. There are fading photos of stiffly posed people whose names you don't know. Their expressions suggest that they were posing for a camera for the first time in their lives—which they very well might have been.

Their manner of dress is not of this era. The men are wearing suits with jackets too tight and pants too short. Most have mustaches or even long beards. The women wear their hair tightly wound, and their long black dresses reveal little more than a pair of high button shoes peeking from under the hem. There are workplace shots, too—a dozen or so workers, half smiling behind sewing machines or retail counters. You notice that the men are wearing yarmulkes, even though they're at work.

The documents in the box are even more mysterious. They seem to be official forms, but it's been a long time since anybody has filled out forms with a pen that had to be dipped in ink between sentences. Or if a typewriter was

Just as many Jewish children begin at a young age the rigorous study of the Hebrew language and scriptures, so, too, does the study of genealogy demand hard work, dedication, and a sincere interest in your Jewish roots.

used, it didn't quite hit on all its keys. No laser printing here!

Some of the documents carry the seal of the U.S. Government. They mention citizenship, immigration, or even learning to read and write English. You can't begin to guess at the meaning of other documents. The words are not only in a different language, but also a different alphabet.

What's in the box? A good part of your heritage. What you've discovered is a treasure chest of your family's history. If it has made you curious to learn more about your family, welcome to a large and growing club—a club of amateur genealogists.

What Genealogy Can Do for You

Genealogy is the study of family history. The study starts with you and works backward through the generations of your family as far as you can or want to go.

You study your parents, their parents, and their parents

before them. You study aunts, uncles, and cousins of several generations. You travel the various branches of your family tree, and you are frequently amazed at where they lead.

The object of your study is to learn about these people's lives: where they lived, what work they did, what education they had, what they believed in, what brought them joy and sorrow. You seek to understand them. They are, after all, members of your family.

As you study, you learn of family members you didn't know existed but who have passed numerous gifts of heredity and heritage to you. And you learn more things about the people you do know.

As you study your ancestors, you mentally travel to the places where they lived, tracing backward from your current hometown to other U.S. cities and towns in which members of your family resided. If your family has a typical Jewish American history, the path will take you to one of several major cities, such as New York, Boston, or Baltimore. Each served as a gateway for millions of Jewish immigrants as they entered the United States.

Through books and other sources, your imagination will lead you through the bustling streets, ripe with the odor of borscht and gefilte fish hawked on pushcarts and served in tiny kitchens. At night, you'll try to sleep through the stifling heat of a summer night in an apartment too small, in a bed shared with several siblings.

From there, the trail will likely lead back across the oceans to other nations. There you will visit both world-famous cities and small towns with strange-sounding names. Some of these communities have existed for 1,000 years. Others now exist only in memory. Sadly, many were destroyed in waves of anti-Jewish hatred that sometimes swept those nations. Amazingly, your search may turn up branches of your family who survived such disasters, a discovery that can enrich your life.

It's in the Bible . . .

The first example of Jewish genealogy is in the Old Testament, that part of the Bible written by the ancient Hebrews

Family ties have sustained Jewish families over centuries of persecution and dislocation. As you may know from your own experience, Jewish holidays are important occasions for families to come together and embrace ancient traditions. This Jewish family gathers for the Festival of Succoth in the early twentieth century.

and called The Torah (The Law) by Jews. Chapter after chapter is devoted to telling who "begat" whom, layering family upon family, forming one long genealogical trail that leads all the way back to Creation.

As the people mentioned seem to have little importance other than as links to later parts of the story, why has so much space been spent on this strange accounting?

The answer seems to be that the Jews understood early on that one of the best ways to keep their faith strong and alive was to link it to family. According to Arthur Kurzweil, author of one of the best books on Jewish American genealogy,[1] "there's no question that, within the Jewish

---

[1] Arthur Kurzweil, *From Generation to Generation: How to Trace Your Jewish Genealogy and Personal History* (New York: HarperCollins, 1994).

tradition, the central idea is that of *family*—keeping it together, and using it as a force for righteous living."

Or as a rabbi told Kurzweil, "If our belief is only of our own thinking, someone could convince us to change it. If our belief is only that of our ancestors, it would not involve us. But if our belief is both ours *and* our ancestors', then our faith will be strong."

Not History—Personal History

But knowing your family's history will also convey more personal rewards, including a better knowledge of who you are. You may discover, for example, where your physical features came from: whether your family is generally tall or short; thin or *zaftig*; large-boned or small; high-voiced or low. Is your family the kind that cries and hugs openly at special occasions? Emotional patterns and social behavior can be a product of background.

You may also come to a better understanding of family customs, traditions, and values: why your parents are willing to sacrifice to send you to that certain college, for instance, even though others are less expensive and all your friends are headed to them. You may learn why family members took up the work they do. Certain highly skilled trades, such as dealing in jewelry, have been in Jewish families for generations.

And why are members of your family willing—or not willing—to take risks such as investing money? These attitudes also are taught from generation to generation and are often shaped by conditions families have lived through in the past. If your family is conservative about money, don't be surprised to find that your forebears lived through economic troubles or political revolutions in some part of the world. Hard-learned lessons from surviving those experiences were then incorporated into the lives of the generations that followed.

Even the food on your dinner table may be ordered up by family history. Does the menu include *pirogi*, a Russian dish, or the Greek favorite, *baklava*? Or a kind of spinach pie first

Your ancestors may be among the many Jewish refugees who fled persecution in Nazi Germany, like Trudel Levy and Emilia Herz, pictured above, who arrived in New York in 1938.

served in Spain centuries ago? These may have come from some currently fashionable cookbook. But they may also have been taught by parent to child and have been in your family for ages.

In short, much of what you are and how you live comes to you by way of the past. By knowing that past, you can better understand the present and better pass your heritage to your children.

Not an Easy Process

Though the rewards of studying genealogy may be great, gaining the knowledge is not always easy. In the best of cases the past lies buried; the farther back you go, the deeper you have to dig to get to it. People's memories fade, and those you most want to talk to may be out of reach. Documents are lost, and the documents that lead to them get lost, too. These are all common problems for genealogists.

But Jewish American genealogists also have to deal with special difficulties. Many documents will be in Yiddish, Hebrew, German, Russian, or other languages. And because the Jews often moved, or were forced to move, records may be scattered.

Names may have been changed as Jewish immigrants sought to be more "native" in their new host nations. "Weisskopf" may have become "Wise," or "Moshe" may have become "Max." In some cases, border officials unable to pronounce or spell the names of immigrants simply made up new names to write on the entry forms. Weisskopf may have become Smith!

Finally, the murder of millions of Jews by the Nazis during World War II—and earlier hate crimes, as well—caused huge gaps in family history. Entire branches of some families were wiped out.

Nevertheless, it's amazing how much you can find, often going no farther than your own attic to find it. There are two basic ways of doing it:

- Interview people who've lived through the period you want to study, especially the older members of your family.
- Examine books and other written records from and about the period you want to study, and physical items such as photographs or household items used in that period.

The Costs of Genealogical Research

Poring through family albums, files, and documents and collecting the thoughts and memories of family members will probably cost you nothing at all. But as your search progresses, you will find that you can potentially spend a lot of money—on photocopies, stamps, membership in genealogical organizations, phone calls, books, supplies, travel, computer software. Some people dedicated to exploring their family history even hire professional genealogists to pursue difficult research tasks such as accessing out-of-state or overseas records.

Your search need not be expensive, however. Many of the expenses incurred by family historians are avoidable if you are resourceful and creative and, in some cases, willing to expend a little more time and effort. Here are some cost-saving tips:

- Borrow library materials, rather than buying books, as much as possible. This may mean spending more time taking notes, but books can be extremely costly and are probably not worth the expense, especially if you are using only a few chapters or sections of a book. Many of the microfilmed records you need may also be available at your library or a Family History Center (which will be discussed later in this book). If the books or microfilm you need are not available at your library, talk to your librarian about the possibility of borrowing or renting them from another library. Librarians will be eager to help you find the materials you need.
- If the records you need are located in another state,

you may be able to order microfilmed records instead of making the trip yourself. If you have friends or relatives who live in the area where the records are located, ask them if they might be able to look up the records for you.

- Ask your siblings, parents, or friends if they might have any boxes, files, or audio/visual equipment they can donate to your project.
- Use plain—even recycled—paper for recording your information instead of preprinted forms.
- If you are interested in visiting a particular ancestral location or can only complete a step in your research by conducting the research on-site, suggest to your parents that this travel be incorporated in your next family vacation.

Relatives may be willing to contribute a small amount to your project, if approached carefully. Be sure that you are serious about the project—people will not want to donate money to a halfhearted effort. Tell them what they can expect to gain from their contribution. Promise them a copy of the finished product, for example, or provide them with monthly updates on your progress. You may want to begin your research and have some results in hand before approaching relatives, so that they can see how fascinating your project can potentially be. Make a list of the expenses you expect to incur so relatives can see why their help is needed, and also so that they can get an idea of the amount they might donate. Of course, if your project is interrupted, canceled, or postponed, be sure to return any donations you have not used toward the project.

Adoptees and Children of Single-Parent Families

There are now many "typical" kinds of families. One out of every four U.S. families with children is headed by a single parent. That is three times the number of such families just ten years ago. One-third to half of all marriages end in divorce and have led to many "blended" families with children from both prior marriages. Adoption is increasingly common. And many children today are raised by grandparents, aunts, uncles, or family friends.

This is not a new phenomenon. Many European parents, including Jewish parents, sent their children to be cared for by family friends in the United States when economic conditions at home worsened or war broke out. The parents planned to follow later. My father was sent from Russia to live with a man our family still calls "Uncle Benjamin," a family friend in New York. Benjamin took my father on as an apprentice in his jewelry business. Apprenticeship was a common custom in Europe. Benjamin let his apprentice sleep in the loft over the shop. When Benjamin retired, he gave his shop to my father as a gift, starting a new family tradition of participation in the jewelry business. This uncle who wasn't an uncle changed the course of our family's history.

If you live in a single-parent family, you may decide to research only one family line. This is still a challenging and fully rewarding project. Even if you are not in contact with one of your parents, you may be able to obtain information about that parent from another relative.

If you are adopted and want to identify your birth parents, the situation is somewhat different. There are legal paths to follow, but in almost every state they are closed to anyone under eighteen. Even after you reach eighteen, you may need the help of a lawyer to see your adoption records. In certain situations, however, such as a medical emergency requiring a genetic history, records can be opened earlier.

It is possible that your adoptive parents have some basic information about your birth parents. Approach them about this with great care. Be sure they understand that your aim is to learn your biological history, not to replace them as your parents. There are books and organizations to help you understand the process and the emotions involved.

It may be best to wait until you're legally an adult before taking on this quest. Consider researching the history of your adoptive family. Tracing it through the generations may give you a stronger sense of your role in the family of which you are now a part.

Resources

STARTING YOUR EXPLORATION

Blume, Judy. *Are You There, God? It's Me, Margaret.*
New York: Bradbury, 1970.

In this classic coming-of-age novel, Margaret is an eleven-year-old girl from suburban New Jersey with a lot of questions and worries. Her father is Jewish, her mother Christian. Her Jewish grandmother wants her to have Jewish boyfriends; her Christian grandparents disowned her mother because she married a Jew. These are among the many concerns on Margaret's mind.

Brownstone, David M. *The Jewish-American Heritage.*
New York: Facts on File, 1988.

Firsthand accounts and period illustrations are used to describe the history of Jewish Americans, their reasons for immigrating, and their contributions to American culture.

Freedman, E. B., et al. *What Does Being Jewish Mean? Read-Aloud Responses to Questions Jewish Children Ask About History, Culture, and Religion.*
New York: Prentice Hall, 1991.

If you have questions about your Jewish identity or simply want to know the definition of words you've heard at your synagogue, consult this sourcebook written by an orthodox rabbi. It covers topics such as Bible stories, Jewish customs, and the history of Israel.

Meltzer, Milton. *Starting From Home: A Writer's Beginnings.* **New York: Viking, 1988.**

Prolific author Meltzer, the son of Jewish immigrants who settled in Worcester, Massachusetts, tells his life story in the context of social and political events of the 1920s and 1930s.

Moline, Jack. *Growing Up Jewish; or, Why Is This Book Different from All Other Books?* New York: Penguin, 1987.

Written by a rabbi, this book provides a humorous look at being Jewish today. The author targets such topics as "chicken, the wonder food" and circumcision.

Muggamin, Howard. *The Jewish Americans.* Broomall, PA: Chelsea House, 1995.

Illustrated with photographs, this volume examines the culture and achievements of Jewish Americans.

Potok, Chaim. *The Chosen.* New York: Knopf, 1967.

Made into a feature film, this novel tells the story of the friendship between two Orthodox Jewish boys.

Press, D. *Jewish Americans.* North Bellmore, NY: Benchmark Books, 1995.

This examination of Jewish American culture looks at issues such as family and community values, as well as the importance of religion, celebrations, and special social customs.

Schwartz, Howard. *Miriam's Tambourine: Jewish Folktales from around the World.* New York: Free Press, 1986.

Fifty tales from around the world are evidence of the rich Jewish folklore tradition.

Simon, Kate. *A Wider World: Portraits in Adolescence.* New York: HarperCollins, 1986.

Simon recounts her childhood in New York City during the Depression, describing her encounters with friends, family, work, and school.

Simon, Neil. *Brighton Beach Memoirs*. **New York: Random House, 1984.**

An entertaining and amusing play about a Depression-era Jewish family in Brooklyn. Fifteen-year-old Eugene is the protagonist.

Strom, Yale. *A Tree Still Stands: Jewish Youth in Eastern Europe Today*. **New York: Putnam/Philomel, 1990.**

Jewish youths from Poland and other countries tell their stories, which are illustrated with photo essays.

INFORMATION ABOUT ADOPTION

Askin, Jayne, and Davis, Molly. *Search: A Handbook for Adoptees and Birthparents*, **2d ed. Phoenix, AZ: Oryx Press, 1992.**

This reference work provides sources for adoptee searches, including advice on laws and family issues.

People Searching News.

Bimonthly newsletter that serves both adoptees and birth parents trying to connect. Contact address is:
J. E. Carlson and Associates
P.O. Box 22611
Ft. Lauderdale, FL 33335
305-370-7100

Sadler, Judith DeBoard. *Families in Transition: An Annotated Bibliography*. **Hamden, CT: Archon Books, 1988.**

A comprehensive reference to find out what you need to know about nontraditional families, including addresses of support groups.

Witherspoon, Mary Ruth. "How to Conduct an Adoption Search." *Everton's Genealogical Helper*, **July/August, 1994.**

Details the how-tos of conducting a search for one's birth family. The author was successful: she found 300 relatives.

The following support groups exist to help draw together people from nontraditional family situations. They are not specific to religion.

Adoptees and Birthparents in Search
P.O. Box 5551
West Columbia, SC 29171

Adoptees' Liberty Movement Association (ALMA)
P.O. Box 154, Washington Bridge Station
New York, NY 10003

Adoptive Families of America
3333 Highway 100 North
Minneapolis, MN 55422

Concerned United Birth Parents
200 Walker Street
Des Moines, IA 50317

International Soundex Reunion Registry
P.O. Box 2312
Carson City, NV 89702

Soundex is a system designed to help people who know how to pronounce a family name, but not its spelling. This is a common problem with names generated from languages having different alphabets or spelling rules.

National Adoption Information Clearinghouse
11426 Rockville Pike
Rockville, MD 20852

Chapter 2

In the Beginning . . .

Where does your family fit within the 4,000-year story of Judaism, not only in time but in terms of what Jews believe is important and what defines them as Jews?

To understand your personal history, it helps to first understand the history of the Jewish people. It is within that framework that your forebears have made their contribution. It is that framework that defines what you are and why you believe as you do today.

Enter the *Ivriim* (Hebrews)

Let's start by making it clear that no one really knows the complete history of the people now called the Jews—only that it is very long and began more than 1,000 years before the word *Jew* was used.

Scholars believe that this ancient people, known first as *Ivriim* (the English version is "Hebrews," and the meaning is "those who cross over the river"), were one of many desert tribes in the area northeast of modern Israel. It's an area archaeologists call Mesopotamia.

At some point, about 4,000 years ago, a tribal leader named Abraham underwent a religious experience. He claimed to have heard the voice of God. The voice instructed him to make a sacrifice of his son, Isaac, a common practice at the time.

Abraham prepared to do as he had been told. He took the child to a nearby mountain and prepared an altar, placing his son upon it. Then, with the knife just above his son, an angel appeared and told Abraham that God had withdrawn the child's death sentence. Abraham was told to kill a ram instead.

God had been testing Abraham's faith. Once that faith was proven, Abraham was told that, if his descendants followed God's way, they would flourish and become God's "Chosen" people. Those people are the Jews. The promise has since been known as The Covenant.

There is, of course, no scientific way of knowing if the story is true. Like so much in religion, it is taken on faith. But one thing we do know: At the time of Abraham, it was commonly believed that there were separate gods for everything from the rivers to the sun. Abraham and his descendants brought forth the concept of one God. This belief is now shared by some of the world's largest religions. Many still consider the idea of one God, which is called monotheism, the greatest gift the Jews have given to the world.

In the centuries that followed, Abraham's people did indeed prosper and multiply into twelve great families, or tribes, each named after a son of Jacob or Joseph, Abraham's grandson and great-grandson, respectively. They lived in the region that now includes the State of Israel (which is itself named after one of Abraham's descendants). In time, however, crop failures led them to move south to Egypt. There, they eventually became enslaved.

Their rescuer was, of course, Moses, one of the greatest and most mysterious personalities in the Old Testament. No one knows if he was actually placed in a reed basket by his Hebrew mother and rescued by an Egyptian princess, as the Bible tells us. Some who have studied the period think he may even have been an Egyptian, as his name is similar to Thut-Mose, an Egyptian Pharaoh.

No one really knows if there were ten plagues, followed by an incredible escape through the parted waters of the Red Sea. Egyptian records of the time don't hint at anything unusual. But one thing is known: Sometime during that period, the Hebrews received the great body of law called The Ten Commandments—ten simple statements that lay out how people of good will should live together without killing, stealing, or cheating, and by keeping faith in God and each other. The Ten Commandments are at the heart of modern law as it is practiced around the world. This was the second great gift given by Judaism to the world.

Moses left another legacy: He brought his people back from Egypt to the land of Abraham and his descendants, called the Promised Land. The biblical nation of Israel was established there. Warriors, judges, prophets, kings, heroes, and evildoers then played out a 1,000-year drama there. They took the nation from greatness to ruin—several times.

Diaspora

In the end, Israel was conquered and the Israelites scattered among many nations. This happening has become known as the Diaspora, or dispersion. Ten of the twelve ancient families or tribes disappeared into the mists of time. Of the two that remained, one tribe, Judah, gave its name to the land, Judea, and the people, the Jews. Eventually, most people in this group were forced out too.

The small remnant of Jews remaining in the Promised Land continued to make history. Conquered first by the Greeks, and then the Romans, the Jews kept their faith strong. They were constantly in rebellion.

At this time there arose a young man who preached a message of peace and brotherhood but also called himself the Son of God. He was executed by Roman soldiers. They put him to death in the manner of the time by nailing him to a wooden cross—crucifixion.

The young man's name was Jesus. And his message, picked up first by Jews and then non-Jews, spread across the earth. Though the Jews refused to accept Jesus—or anyone else—as the Son of God, they recognized many of Jesus' ideas of fair treatment to others and help for those less fortunate. And the Jews who did accept Jesus played a part in a third great change in the world: the birth of a new religion called Christianity.

The Past and Your Life

You can see the effects of this first 2,000 years of Jewish history on the way you live today. The Covenant and the

The aftermath of World War II brought Jews from all over the world to the United States in pursuit of freedom to practice their religion. Rabbi User Weinberger, his wife, Feodora, and their family of twelve children arrived in the United States from Czechoslovakia in 1949.

Law, as expressed in the Commandments, are at the heart of the Jewish family's beliefs and shape its behaviors and attitudes to the present day.

The Diaspora is important because it was not until the birth of the twentieth-century State of Israel that the Jews again had a homeland. Instead, they lived among others, moving constantly, often because they were forced to move. This is why your family likely comes from one of the nations of Eastern Europe, or Spain, or several nations in turn. And the complex relationship between Jews and Christians, along with other groups such as the Muslims, has been a driving force behind where Jews lived and how they've lived for centuries.

We'll see how these forces play out in later chapters.

The story of the Jews as told in the Bible is important for another reason. "The Jewish people are a family," writes Kurzweil, "and the Bible is the beginning of the story of the family. [Understanding this] helps to maintain us as a group."

Resources

JEWISH HISTORY

Ausubel, Nathan. *Pictorial History of the Jewish People.* **New York: Crown Publishers, 1953.**

An aged but heavily illustrated account that's as well worth looking at as it is reading.

Borchaisenius, Paul. *The History of the Jews.* **New York: Simon & Schuster, 1965.**

A five-volume set that takes history from the Bible through the present day. The author was a Danish pastor who was active in helping Jews escape from the Nazis; he offers much personal comment on Jewish strengths as well as personal experiences.

De Lange, Nicholas. *Atlas of the Jewish World.* **Washington, DC: Facts on File, 1984.**

Presents maps, photos, and text to tour key locales of Jewish history in the biblical period, today, and periods in between. Includes a time line of Jewish history and an index.

Dimont, Max I. *Jews, God and History.* **New York: New American Library, 1962.**

Writing in a highly personal style, Dimont covers the sweep of time from the Bible to modern Israel like a news reporter, filling in small details that make history come alive.

Eban, Abba. *Heritage: Civilization and the Jews.* **New York: Summit Books, 1994.**

Written by one of Israel's most prominent leaders, this history recounts the Jews' long journey from Mesopotamia to modern Israel and concentrates on how "such a small people have had such a huge influence" in law, politics, and other areas.

———. *My People: The Story of the Jews*. New York: Random House, 1984.

Surveys two periods in particular: the Middle Ages and the Zionist, or return-to-Israel period, ending in the birth of modern Israel.

Holtz, Barry W., ed. *Back to the Sources*. New York: Summit Books, 1984.

A guide to the classic Jewish books, including the Bible, the Talmud, and Hasidic writings. The author sets the context and relates it to sample writings. Glossary.

Martin, Gilbert. *Atlas of Jewish History*. New York: William Morrow, 1993.

More than 120 maps cover historical sites, battlegrounds, and migrations of the Jews from biblical times to the founding of the State of Israel.

Roth, Cecil. *A History of the Jews from Earliest Times Through the Six-Day War*. New York: Schocken Books, 1970.

Called "the best one-volume history of the Jews in English."

———, and Wigoder, Jeffrey, eds. *Encyclopedia Judaica*. Keter, 1972.

This sixteen-volume work has thousands of articles, more than 11 million words, and 8,000 illustrations. On issues where there is controversy, both sides are presented.

Steinberg, Milton. *Basic Judaism*. New York: Harcourt Brace Jovanovich, 1975.

Written by a rabbi, this work explains Jewish ideals, beliefs, practices, rituals, and daily life.

Williams, Jay G. *Judaism.* **Wheaton, IL: Theosophical Publishing House, 1980.**

This work explores how Jews interacted with many ancient cultures, including those of Cyprus, Rome, Spain, and the Islamic world.

SPECIAL HISTORICAL TOPICS

Baron, Salo W., Arcadius, Kahan, et al. *Economic History of the Jews.* **New York: Schocken Books, 1976.**

An examination of Jewish history from the standpoint of business and industry. Covers farming, diamonds and goldsmithing, retailing, textiles, even peddling.

Birnbaum, Philip. *Encyclopedia of Jewish Concepts.* **Hebrew Publishing, 1979.**

Defines the Jewish views of the Bible, worship, mourning, law, and some 1,600 other subjects. Arranged alphabetically and indexed in both English and Hebrew.

———, ed. *The New Treasury of Judaism.* **New York: Sanhedrin Press, 1977.**

Selection of actual writings from the Bible, the Talmud, and key rabbis. Each is introduced and formatted for easy reading.

Canton, Norman F. *The Sacred Chain.* **New York: HarperCollins, 1994.**

Discussion of how remembering and honoring Jewish ideals and traditions kept the Jews' identity intact no matter in what culture they settled.

De Breffny, Brian. *The Synagogue.* **New York: Macmillan, 1978.**

Illustrated guide to 2,500 years of sacred buildings. Explains differences between synagogues of various eras and how they reflected their periods.

This forty-volume series covers each book of the Bible in a separate volume.

Asimov, Isaac. *Asimov's Guide to the Bible: The Old Testament.* **New York: Avon Books, 1971.**

Best known for his science fiction, Asimov here discusses what really may have happened to inspire stories such as that of the Great Flood.

Avigad, Nahman. *Discovering Jerusalem.* **London: Nelson, 1983.**

A top archaeologist describes the excavations done among the ruins of the old Jewish Quarter of the city. Many photos.

Finkelstein, Louis. *Akiba: Scholar, Saint and Martyr.* **New York: Atheneum, 1970.**

Most Jews have heard the expression "Rabbi Akiba said . . ." Here's the story of the great leader who lived in Jerusalem during Roman times and was executed for the "crime" of teaching the Torah.

Fox, Everett, tr. *In the Beginning: A New English Rendition of the Book of Genesis.* **New York: Schocken Books, 1983.**

The ancients transmitted the Bible from generation to generation as a series of spoken sermons, fables, and stories. This special translation of Genesis is designed to be read aloud in the same way.

Josephus, Flavius. *The Jewish War.* **Translated by Goalya Cornfeld. New York: Zondervan, 1982.**

News-like reporting on the rebellion of the Jews against their Roman conquerors.

Neil, William, and Rasmussen, B. H., tr. *The Bible as History.* **New York: William Morrow, 1981.**

How accurate is the Bible? This is a study of the archaeological evidence that supports—and doesn't support—the familiar stories.

Pearlman, Moshe. *The Zealots of Masada: Story of a Dig.* **New York: Scribner, 1967.**

Find out what archaeologists learned when they studied Israel's Masada. This book explains the process and results, and how the physical evidence relates to the legend. Illustrated.

Samuel, Maurice. *Certain People of the Book.* **New York: UAHC Press, 1977.**

Samuel looks at biblical personalities, likeable or not, and explores their interactions as people.

Sarna, Nahum M. *Exploring Exodus: The Heritage of Biblical Israel.* **New York: Schocken Books, 1986.**

Is there one major event that forever changed your way of thinking? Sarna thinks that for Jews that event is the Passover. This volume explores how it touches our lives.

Steinsaltz, Adin. *Biblical Images: Men and Women of the Book.* **New York: Basic Books, 1984.**

Based on an Israeli radio series, this book highlights twenty-five key individuals of Bible history.

Wilson, Edmund. *The Dead Sea Scrolls.* **New York: Farrar, Straus, & Giroux, 1978.**

Explains how the scrolls were found and what they tell us about life and Judaism 2,000 years ago.

FILMS

Ben Hur, **1956. Directed by William Wyler.**

Fictional tale of a Jewish prince who lived at the time Rome controlled Judea and Jesus was teaching. Actually more a New Testament tale, *Ben Hur* is interesting for its portrait of Jewish life under the Romans and for the chariot race scene, for which an entire arena was built.

The Ten Commandments, 1956. Directed by Cecil B. DeMille.

The biggest film spectacle ever made when it was introduced. It was also the Best Picture of 1956.

Chapter 3
The Jewish Diaspora

From the time they were scattered like the wind across many nations, the Jews embarked on a history very different from that of most other peoples. Not for centuries would Jewish history be a story of kings and generals, battles and alliances. Instead it became a history of ideas, and a story of how a small group found ways to survive and even thrive among others who often held power over their lives.

Make no mistake about it, the Jews are a small group. Even today, they number fewer than 20 million in a world population of more than 5 billion. The United States has as large a Jewish population as any nation, including Israel, but Jews still form just over 2 percent of the total population. That's 6 million Jews out of 260 million Americans.

Judaism is often considered one of America's three great religions (Catholicism and Protestantism are the other two). That's a tribute to the power of Jewish ideas and the achievements of American Jews. But in numerical terms, Jews are outnumbered by Americans of other faiths by some forty to one.

In the United States, being "outnumbered" in this way is not a problem. Freedom of religion and the rights of minorities are protected by law (although incidents of anti-Semitism, discrimination, and violence toward Jews still occur in this country). But some nations where Jews have lived have had an "official religion," backed by the government. As your family history may tell you, being Jewish in these nations has often turned out to be a terrible problem.

Jews of the Middle Ages

From about the time the Roman Empire ended to when America won its freedom—some 1,300 years—the Jews of the Diaspora moved out of the Middle East and spread throughout large parts of Europe. There were major settlements in Spain and Eastern Europe, and smaller communities elsewhere.

Jews were massacred in western Europe for the "crime" of being Jewish. In 1245, the Lateran Council, a council of the Roman Catholic Church, required Jews to wear skullcaps (yarmulke) to distinguish them as Jews.

In 1290, Edward I of England banished the Jews from England and confiscated their property. Many moved to northern France and Germany. In France, the Jews were expelled and recalled four times between 1132 and 1321. Jews were not allowed to own land or become members of Christian trade or craft guilds in medieval western Europe. The Black Death, or black plague, was even blamed on Jews in 1348, and tens of thousands were burned for this "crime."

Poland became something of a refuge for western European Jews fleeing Christian persecution. From the fourteenth century to the seventeenth century, Jews in Poland and nearby Lithuania enjoyed rights and freedoms they had been denied in western Europe. The majority had come to Poland or Lithuania from Germany. The Polish-Lithuanian Jewish community produced some of the world's finest scholarship of the Talmud, the authoritative body of the Jewish tradition.

Lacking land of their own in Europe, the Jews found work in the growing cities. They became merchants and bankers and specialized in certain trades. In some lands, the contributions of Jewish residents were appreciated. But too often, their different ways were hated and feared, and their refusal to join the national church was seen as treasonous. Jews were labeled "unbelievers" and worse. They were rumored to use Christian blood for their Passover preparations and to bring disease and famine.

Many European kingdoms forced all Jews to wear "badges of shame," and attacks on Jewish communities and businesses were frequent. Jews were harassed and tortured in an attempt to get them to change their religion. When that failed, some were burned at the stake.

Even William Shakespeare took his shot at the Jews. A leading character in *The Merchant of Venice* is Shylock, a Jewish moneylender. Depicted as cunning and greedy, Shylock demands payment even if it takes a "pound of flesh."

Other parts of the play seem to excuse Shylock, however, so it's not certain that Shakespeare actually held a negative view of the Jews. In fact, it's not certain he ever actually saw a Jew. All Jews had been expelled from England centuries before the play was written. They were not officially allowed to return until the 1650s.

The Middle Ages (500–1500 AD) were years when strong religious feelings swept through Europe. Any group that wished to practice its own religion instead of the state religion was labeled undesirable by officials and might be accused of doing the devil's work by the more superstitious masses. France, Portugal, and several Italian states followed England in casting out the Jews. After a horrible period of terror and torture called the Inquisition, Spain forced them to leave or be killed in 1492. This brought to an end one of the largest, most advanced Jewish communities in the world.

It is suspected, though not proved, that some of the crew of Columbus's ships were Jews escaping the Inquisition. It is known that some of the first European settlers of Spanish-controlled South America were Jews.

Most Jews cast out of Europe, however, moved east toward Russia. They found the Russian czar didn't want them either. His government drew a line beyond which no Jew could settle. The area where Jews were permitted to reside later became known as The Pale of Settlement.

Evicted from western Europe, and barred from Russia, many of the migrants settled in parts of Germany and Poland.

Jews in Spain

A significant number of Jews came under Muslim rule as Islam expanded rapidly in the seventh and eighth centuries.

Jewish communities have existed in Morocco since the eighth century. In this undated photo, a rabbi in Fez, Morocco, touches the Great Holy Book, the Sefer.

Within Muslim communities, Jews were allowed to maintain autonomy over their religious affairs as long as they paid tribute to Muslim rulers. From the eighth to the mid-twelfth centuries, Jews enjoyed a period of relative security and prosperity under Muslim rule in Spain in such communities as Toledo, Córdoba, and Granada. The Jewish-Muslim culture of Spain was marked by high levels of creativity and industriousness, and the literature, architecture, scholarship, and craftmanship it produced contributed greatly to the development of Spanish and European civilization. During the eleventh and twelfth centuries, however, anti-Semitism began to rear its head as Spain was reconquered by the Christians.

Expulsion from Spain and the Path to North America

The Ottoman Empire, Morocco, and the Netherlands were among the places that welcomed the Jews who were expelled from Spain in 1492. Jews spread throughout the Mediterranean world, where some communities spoke a Judeo-Spanish language known as Judezmo or Ladino. This language is still spoken today by some Jewish communities, particularly in Bulgaria, Greece, and Turkey. In the Ottoman Empire (a Muslim Turkish empire whose conquered territories included present-day Iraq, Egypt, Syria, and the Balkan Peninsula), Jews rose to positions of power and generally grew prosperous in the sixteenth century. However, the decline of the Ottoman Empire in the seventeenth century also spelled economic decline for the Jews.

Italy was another destination for Jews who had been expelled from Spain. Urbino, Venice, Ferrara, Florence, Spoleto, Siena, Ancona, and Mantua were among the central Italian cities with thriving Jewish communities during the sixteenth century. The Jews were expelled from southern Italy, however, during this same century. Many came to the Americas, especially Dutch Brazil. When Brazil came under Portugese rule in 1654, the Jews emigrated to the Dutch West Indies and North America.

The Jews were firmly established in the Netherlands by the early seventeenth century. By 1657 they were allowed to apply for Dutch citizenship, though not on completely equal terms with native Dutch citizens. Sephardim (the branch of European Jews who had settled in Spain and Portugal) made up the majority of Jews in Amsterdam during most of the seventeenth century, until they were outnumbered by an influx of Ashkenazim (the branch of eastern European, Yiddish-speaking Jews) fleeing Cossack (Russian peasant soldiers who served the czars) massacres in Poland.

Some Jews emigrated from the Netherlands to the Dutch West Indies and Surinam, and from there to North America, with most settling in New Amsterdam (which soon became New York) and Newport, Rhode Island.

The Shtetl and the Ghetto

Wherever they settled, Jews usually formed small communities of their own, sometimes called shtetls. Many cities had "Jewish streets," often walled off from the rest of the community. The Judeo-Italian term for such an area was "ghetto."

Within each shtetl or ghetto, the Jews ruled themselves, making their own laws based on the Torah and on the Talmud, the series of writings that explained what the Torah meant. Laws were enforced by special Jewish courts, with rabbis sitting in judgment and basing their decisions on the holy writings.

Jewish law could be very different from that of surrounding communities. In some nations, it was common at the time for a man to have several wives and to divorce them as he pleased. Jewish law has forbidden polygamy for the last 1,000 years, and divorce was allowed only if the marriage could not be saved and the divorced person was given money to live on. "The Jewish family was changed," said one writer, "from something at a man's whim into a legal partnership between a couple, bound by the will of both." This is the view of marriage most people, Jews and non-Jews, hold today.

The Lublin, Poland, shtetl of the early nineteenth century was an example of an enclosed Jewish neighborhood.

Jewish communities also had their own schools. Those at the highest level were called, as they are now, yeshivas. The name, it is said, comes from the expression, "Moses *yashav* [sat] to judge the people." Rabbis and students labored to understand the Torah and Talmud and explain them to their flocks. Questions came from the common citizens and were debated; then answers called *responsa* were issued.

To Jews, education was a mark of honor at a time when most other Europeans could neither read nor write nor felt the need to learn. One twelfth-century observer summed up the Jews' feelings about learning: "No matter how poor, if a Jew has ten sons," he wrote, "he will put them all to letters [educate them], and not only his sons, but also his daughters."

Rabbis were the celebrities of their day. Some boasted of their own followings, as music or sports stars do today. Students traveled long and far for the privilege of studying with a favored rabbi.

It was in approximately 1100 AD that European Jews invented their own language, popularly called Yiddish. By the 1700s, it was widely spoken by eastern European Jews. The words are mostly German but written with Hebrew letters. Yiddish migrated with the Jews. As it did, words of other languages entered the Yiddish vocabulary. If any of your relatives speak the language, listen for the occasional English word or phrase mixed into what otherwise sounds like German.

Sephardim and Ashkenazim

As the Jews spread through Europe and the Middle East, clearly defined branches of Judaism developed, each with its own language and customs, reflecting the culture of their adopted lands. If your family hails from Jewish settlements in Spain, Portugal, and other lands bordering the Mediterranean, they belong to the Sephardic branch. They are often darker-skinned than their northern counterparts and may speak Spanish. Those who settled in more northern and eastern parts of Europe are called Ashkenazic Jews. There is also a Mediterranean branch of Judaism, whose members settled in Egypt, Turkey, Iran, and other lands of the East.

The great majority of Jewish Americans are Ashkenazim. But whichever segment your family descended from, you can probably see many of the attitudes of the past reflected in their attitudes today. Wherever they have wandered, Jews have always carried with them strong faith, an independent spirit, and a high regard for work and education.

There has been one other great theme in Jewish history: Wherever they were, Jews dreamed of Israel as their homeland. Even today, each Passover seder, the ceremonial meal commemorating the Exodus, ends with the saying, "Next year in Jerusalem."

Jewish Emancipation and Assimilation

The emancipation (granting of freedom) of Jews was proclaimed in parts of present-day Germany after the Revolution of 1848. The revolution's liberating effects on Jews were also felt in Sweden, Denmark, and Greece. Following the French Revolution, the French National Assembly voted for full emancipation of Jews in 1791. Other European countries followed in granting the Jews full equality: Britain in 1858, Austria in 1867, Italy in 1870, and 1871 in the German Empire. However, Jews were not emancipated until 1917 in Russia (and still faced persecution during the civil war) and not until 1919 in Romania.

The difficulties the Jews had faced over the centuries in Europe led to a movement among some Jews to make changes in Jewish life and identity. The movement, called Haskalah ("enlightenment" in Hebrew), began in Germany and was the brainchild of the German Jewish philosopher Moses Mendelssohn. The movement called for a secularization of Jewish life, a shift to secular (nonreligious) learning, a focus on aesthetics (a branch of philosophy concerning nature, creation, and the appreciation of beauty), and linguistic assimilation. Secularization and assimilation movements occurred throughout Europe, particularly after a wave of pogroms (organized massacres) in Eastern Europe in 1881. The Reform movement, for example, proposed a Judaism that focused on ethical concerns rather than adherence to traditional Jewish law. Today, many American Jews consider themselves Reform Jews.

Jewish Communities Around the World

Outside of the United States and Israel, significant Jewish communities exist in the former Soviet Union, Great Britain, Canada, France, and Argentina. In China, the Jewish presence can be traced back to the eighth century, and small communities of Jews exist today in Beijing, Hangzhou, Yinchuan, Nanjing, and Guangzhou. A very small Jewish community still exists in Kaifeng; it was founded in the eleventh century when seventy Jewish families emigrated from Persia.

One of the most publicized cases of Jewish dispersal in recent years was the airlifting of thousands of Ethiopian Jews out of Ethiopia in the face of famine and political instability, first in 1984 and then in 1991. They were resettled in Israel and the United States.

Resources

JEWS IN THE MIDDLE AGES

Abrahams, Israel. *Jewish Life in the Middle Ages*. **New York: Atheneum, 1978.**

> Daily life, business, and the role of the synagogue are explained in this account of how Jews lived in a time when the church ruled the state and only the official religion was tolerated.

Ashtor, Eliyahu. *The Jews of Moslem Spain*, **3 vols. New York: Jewish Publication Society, 1974–84.**

> Concentrates on how Sephardic Jews lived when Spain was largely under Muslim control. The two communities coexisted peacefully, and the period saw a flowering of the arts and sciences as a result of their fruitful interaction.

Heschel, Abraham Joshua. *Maimonides*. **New York: Farrar, Straus & Giroux 1982.**

> The rabbi known as Maimonides lived in the twelfth century and was the source of many ideas adopted by Jewish communities since. This work explores his life, with a detailed description of his final days.

Marcus, Jacob R. *The Jew in the Medieval World*. **Westport, CT: Greenwood Press, 1975.**

> Documents generated during 150 years of interaction between Jews and Christian and Muslim communities and their rulers.

Metzger, Therese, and Metzger, Mendel. *Jewish Life in the Middle Ages: Illuminated Hebrew Manuscripts of* *the Thirteenth to Sixteenth Centuries.* **Paris: Alpine Fine Arts, 1982.**

Daily Jewish life is shown in full color, through miniature paintings used to illustrate books during the Middle Ages.

Netanyahu, Benzion. *The Origins of the Inquisition in Fifteenth-Century Spain.* **New York: Random House, 1995.**

Written by an Israeli scholar, this work ties the Inquisition to a larger theme of anti-Semitism that far predated the events in Spain.

Roth, Cecil. *A History of the Marranos.* **New York: Ayer, 1932.**

The Marranos were Sephardic Jews forced to convert during the Spanish Inquisition. Only partly accepted by the Spanish, they were still able to achieve a "Golden Age" in art, literature, and other fields.

Sachar, Howard Morley. *Farewell Espana: The World of the Sephardim Remembered.* **New York: Knopf, 1994.**

Comprehensive work describing the history and achievements of the Sephardim prior to the expulsion of Spanish Jewry in 1492.

THE JEWISH DIASPORA

Aris, Stephen. *But There Are No Jews in England.* **New York: Stern & Day, 1970.**

Great Britain is home to one of Europe's most influential Jewish communities. This review covers the Jews' history there, with special attention to the years following 1880.

Chaliand, Gérard, and Rageau, Jean-Pierre. *The Penguin Atlas of Diasporas.* **New York: Viking, 1995.**

Included in this reference work is a lengthy chapter on the Jewish Diaspora. Detailed maps trace the movement of the Jewish people throughout history. Time lines and photographs add interest to the text.

Keller, Warner. *Diaspora*. New York: Harcourt, Brace & World, 1966.

Covers the "post-biblical" history of the Jews worldwide, concentrating on Europe, but including Jews in China and the so-called "Black Jews" of India.

Lewis, Bernard. *The Jews of Islam*. Princeton: Princeton University Press, 1984.

No relationship has been as important to the Jews of late as that with the Muslim peoples. This book traces the link back to the Middle Ages, then follows it to modern Israel.

Pollak, Michael. *Mandarins, Jews, and Missionaries: The Jewish Experience in the Chinese Empire*. Philadelphia: Jewish Publication Society, 1980.

Jews went to China 1,000 years ago, and a synagogue was still operating in the city of Kaifeng as late as the 1800s. This is the story of that community and how it assimilated into Chinese culture.

Ross, Dan. *Acts of Faith: A Journey to the Fringes of Jewish Identity*. New York: St. Martin's Press, 1982.

The "fringes" in this case are Jewish communities in India, Ethiopia, and other outposts of the faith. Under very difficult conditions, many Ethiopian Jews have attempted to return to Israel.

Stillman, Norman A. *The Jews of Arab Lands: a History and Source Book*. Philadelphia: Jewish Publication Society, 1979.

Presents a very accurate and balanced view of Jewish life in Arab nations.

Weisbrot, Robert. *The Jews of Argentina.* **Philadel-phia: Jewish Publication Society, 1979.**

Argentina boasts the fifth-largest Jewish community in the world. This is the story of its development. The bulk of immigration occurred between 1800 and 1914.

Chapter 4
Coming to America

Few, if any, American Jews can trace their families to the days of the Bible or even of the Inquisition. The generation you're most likely to have personal contact with is one that lived in Europe in the 1800s or early 1900s. It's important, therefore, that you have an accurate picture of that world.

The view many Americans have is that of shtetl society as shown in the popular play and film *Fiddler on the Roof*. The portrayal is of simple, God-fearing people, mostly tradesmen and their families, at the mercy of outsiders.

In fact, the world of the Jews of Europe was far more complex. In nations that accepted them as full citizens, such as the Netherlands, Jews held positions at all levels of society. Some reached high office. There were even "Court Jews," advisers to kings and princes. Some families, such as the Rothschilds of banking fame, had great wealth and power. Many others were members of the middle class.

Study, Mitzvoth, and the Evil Eye

Within the Jewish community, ideas differed on how best to serve God. Some clung to the ancient idea that the Jew's goal should be lifelong study and mastery of the Torah and the Talmud. The yeshiva's aim was to fulfill this goal.

But other Jews, equally religious, explored the world of superstition and magical forces of good and evil. Their belief was in the teachings of the *Kabbalah*, said to be a secret writing given to a chosen few at the time all Jews received the Torah. These Jews are known as Kabbalists.

Superstition played a powerful role in the life of the common person. One common belief held that jealous people had the power to place a spell called the "Evil Eye" on those

Hasidic Jews still dress much as their ancestors did in the 1800s; the men wear beards, long coats, and locks of hair called peyot, near their ears.

more fortunate by staring at them in a certain way. Among some traditional Jews, this belief continues. If your grandparents have uttered the expression *kinneahora* in your presence, it's to defend you against the "Evil Eye."

Another religious movement was led by a rabbi known as the Baal Shem Tov, "The Master of the Good Name." He taught that joy, music, and dance were just as important as quiet study and that the true path to God was to perform mitzvoth—good deeds—for others.

The movement begun by the Baal Shem Tov, known as Hasidism, continues today. Hasidic Jews follow the dress and customs of their forebears of the 1800s. The men wear long coats and beards. The women shave their heads at marriage, then wear wigs in public. They walk behind the men and sit apart from them in the synagogue. Young boys grow locks of hair near their ears. Ceremonies are marked by dancing and singing as well as prayer.

Visit a Hasidic neighborhood to get a sense of how some Jewish communities have retained ancient traditions. The largest such area is in the Williamsburg section of Brooklyn, New York. Especially on the Sabbath, when the Hasidim are wearing their most traditional dress, you'll feel as though you've traveled back in time.

The Great Migration

In 1881, terrorists threw a bomb at Alexander II, the czar of Russia, killing him. The assassination was in response to numerous economic and other troubles in Russia. The shock wave from that blast went on to shake every Jew in Europe—and much of the world.

Although only one of the terrorists was Jewish, and she had a minor role in the plot, Russian officials blamed the entire Jewish population for the killing and for all of Russia's troubles.

Acting publicly, the officials passed laws to uproot the Jews, forcing them off lands they'd occupied in the Pale and other regions for centuries. Privately, the word was passed to the police to turn a blind eye to attacks on Jewish communities by local hate groups. In these vicious raids, called pogroms, homes and businesses were burned and Jews were beaten and killed across vast areas of Russia. One official was asked what results these actions might have on nearly 5 million Jews under Russian domination. "One third will move, one third will convert, and one third will die," he answered. Poland and other parts of Eastern Europe were also under Russian domination at this time, and Jews in these regions suffered consequences similar to Jews in Russia.

The "third that moved" moved west. Hundreds of thousands of refugees flooded the cities of Western Europe, swelling Jewish neighborhoods in such places as the East End of London. Some made their lives there, but many others boarded ships headed to the United States.

In the late 1800s and early 1900s, the United States was undergoing fast growth. People were needed to work in new

NEWSPAPER

Entered according to Act of Congress, in the year 1891, by the Judge Publishing Company, in the Office of the Librarian of Congress at Washington.—Entered at the Post-office, New York, N. Y., as Second-class Matter.

ol. LXXIII.]   NEW YORK—FOR THE WEEK ENDING SEPTEMBER 26, 1891.   [Price, 10

This 1891 New York newspaper drawing depicts Russian Jews who have been detained at the New York City barge office. Thousands of Jews fled Russian pogroms and came to the United States.

industries, fill the cities, and occupy lightly populated lands in the Midwest and West.

For these reasons, the government set an "open door" policy for foreigners. Newcomers were welcomed. Almost anyone who could afford a ticket could enter this new "Promised Land."

The first Jewish settlers had actually arrived as early as 1654, in the then Dutch colony of New Amsterdam, which later became New York City. They were Sephardic Jews, and they were as at home among the Dutch in America as among those back in Holland.

German Jews began to arrive soon after, but the numbers were small. There were fewer than 2,000 Jews in America at the time of the Revolutionary War.

By 1860, that number had grown rapidly. There were 150,000 Jewish Americans at the outbreak of the Civil War, and more than 250,000 by 1880.

The great bulk of these newcomers were German immigrants. They entered through East Coast ports, but rapidly moved west, often working as peddlers selling their wares in isolated communities too small to have their own shopping districts.

The tradition of Jews as merchants was strong, and some of the peddler families built their businesses to amazing size. You may be familiar with some of their names—Macy, Gimbel, and Sears-Roebuck.

All this was just a shadow, however, of the tremendous migration the czar had put in motion.

The first wave of Eastern European Jews began to arrive in 1882. They were followed by other family members and friends. The Jewish populations of entire towns headed to the United States. Thousands moved each month.

Steerage and Railroad Flats

There was money to be made in this exodus. Steamship lines packed the cramped and dirty "steerage" cabins at the bottom of their ships—cabins no other passenger would take—with immigrants. Landlords jammed new arrivals into

overcrowded and often unheated apartment buildings called
tenements. Railroad agents collared them on the dock and
shipped them to Chicago, St. Louis, and other midwestern
cities, promising jobs that turned out to be under conditions
of near slavery, if they existed at all.

There was nothing new about all this. The Jews received
the same treatment the Irish and Germans had experienced
before them and many Hispanic and Asian immigrants have
received since. These groups now live in the same neighborhoods in which immigrant Jews lived, such as New
York's Lower East Side.

Once in the United States, the Jews continued to seek the
best education for their children. Jewish children flooded
public schools in the big cities. Crammed into classrooms,
with no knowledge of English when they arrived, they ex-
celled at their work, surprising their teachers.

Living conditions were demanding in a different way. The
typical tenement was the railroad flat, in which the rooms
were lined up like boxcars. Residents had to walk through
other rooms to get to their own, leaving little privacy. Later
came the so-called dumbbell tenement, whose windows
overlooked air shafts rather than the street so that air and
light were limited.

Few families could afford their own apartments. More
often, several shared one table, and sometimes one bed.
Others, too poor to afford any apartment, lived in storage
cellars, the backs of stores, or the streets.

Work was long, hard, and low-paying. One-third of all
Jews worked in the clothing industry, called the garment
trade. Many labored in "sweatshop" clothing factories, bent
over a sewing machine from early morning to late at night.
Factory owners set working hours as they wished, with no
protection from wage or hour laws. "If you don't come in
Sunday," a famous sign read, "don't come in Monday."

Workplace safety was nonexistent. A newspaper reporter
of the time compared the factory machines to the torture
devices of the Inquisition because they mangled fingers in
the same way.

In the early 1900s, many Jewish immigrants worked in clothing factories, bent over their work for long hours and receiving low wages.

Then, in 1910, the Triangle Shirtwaist Company, a dress factory, caught fire. In just eighteen horrific minutes, 146 workers, mostly young Jewish and Italian women, burned to death. Their route to safety had been blocked. The building's owners had not followed the fire codes.

This outrage shook the Jewish community. The *Jewish Daily Forward*, a Yiddish-language newspaper many immigrants read, gave its front page over to a poem:

> Now let us light the holy candles,
> And mark the sorrow
> Of Jewish masses in darkness and poverty
> This is our funeral, our graves, our children. . . .

Workers went on strike for better working conditions and wages. Unions were formed, including the International Ladies' Garment Workers' Union, which is still active today.

Bringing Light to the Darkness

To the darkness and poverty, the Jews brought light. The new immigrants built an incredibly rich culture all their own. Yiddish newspapers and book publishing companies were started. So was Yiddish theater. Its home was around New York's Second Avenue. Many of its stars later succeeded on Broadway and in the Hollywood movie studios. In fact, several of those studios, including MGM and Warner Brothers, were started by Jews.

The great wave of immigrants began to slow when World War I cut off most travel from Europe in 1914. Even so, by 1926, the Jewish American community had grown to more than 4 million people. They now began to move to better neighborhoods of their cities. Lower East Siders migrated to tree-lined avenues of the Bronx, Brooklyn, and Long Island. Chicagoans moved out to Skokie and Evanston, Clevelanders to Shaker Heights. They started and bought businesses and built homes. They vacationed in New York's Catskill Mountains and similar vacationlands in the summer, and in Florida in the winter. They joined the great American middle class.

Your living relatives were and still are the starring characters in this drama. If you want to hear about it as no book can tell it, all you need to do is ask them.

Jewish American Success Stories

Pick almost any field, and you'll find people of Jewish background who have made memorable contributions. And you'll often find that they credit their success to their family and their heritage, both in this country and in lands their ancestors called home. Following is a sampling of success stories in which Jewish culture, custom, heritage, family, and the immigrant experience played major parts.

Kirk Douglas

Douglas was born Issur Danielovitch, son of Russian immigrants who settled in upstate New York. His father had been a horse trader in Europe but in America could find work only as a ragman, a collector of old clothes and junk. The family barely got by. That did not stop Douglas from following his dream in show business, first on the New York stage and then in Hollywood, where he made dozens of films. Millions saw him star in *Spartacus*, as the leader of a slave revolt that took on the might of the Roman Empire. He produced this and other films and later traveled the world on goodwill trips at the request of the U.S. Government.

Douglas gave up his birth name, but never his heritage. "I know in my guts," he wrote in his autobiography, *The Ragman's Son*, "that I'm related to the slaves who escaped bondage in Egypt and that the people trying to turn Israel into a land of milk and honey are my brethren. Being a Jew has been a theme of my whole life."

It's also been a theme of the life of Kirk's eldest son, Michael Douglas, a superstar actor and producer in his own right. Michael has starred in his own TV series and several Hollywood hits. With his father's help, he produced *One Flew Over the Cuckoo's Nest*, Best Picture of 1975. He is extremely proud to be Kirk's son. "When I look in the mirror to see what I am," he has said, "I see my father."

Levi Strauss

Harbor Lob, a peddler by trade, made the journey from Germany to the United States in 1847, one of many thousands of German Jews to come over during that period. His name was changed to Levi Strauss in the process.

Strauss didn't change his trade, however, and soon found himself peddling tents to California gold miners when what they really wanted was a strong pair of pants. Levi cut up the tents and sewed the tough blue fabric into pairs of pants. The fabric, from the city of de Nimes, France, was called denim. The pants were the first blue jeans.

Through much of its history, Levi Strauss & Co. has been a family business. Strauss's brothers, sisters, and stepbrothers built and ran factories worldwide. And Strauss kept his faith as well. Until his death in 1902, he helped to promote the study of Judaism at the University of California.

Henry Alfred Kissinger

Born Heinz Kissinger, in Fürth, Germany, Kissinger learned early in life how government power could do harm in evil hands. When he was just ten, the Nazis took control of Germany, turning his world upside down. He saw his parents persecuted by government officials while he had to avoid the soccer matches he loved for fear of being beaten by the anti-Semitic Nazis. Fortunately for Kissinger, his family escaped to New York before the mass killings of Jews began.

Life in America was not easy. Kissinger's father, a brilliant teacher in Germany, had to work as a bookkeeper, while his witty and highly educated mother served as a cook. Kissinger himself worked in a brush factory and went to night school.

When World War II began, Kissinger entered the U.S. Army, beginning a lengthy career in and around the government. As a German-speaking officer, he helped U.S. troops govern postwar Germany. Following this duty, he attended Harvard University, and then taught world politics there, becoming renowned in the field. In time he was called to the White House as a special adviser to U.S. Presidents Richard Nixon and Gerald Ford.

In that position, Kissinger had his greatest accomplishments. For twenty years, the United States had been at odds with Russia and China. Many feared another world war would break out at any moment, this time fought with nuclear weapons. Kissinger had the courage and know-how to bring the sides together. He made secret trips and negotiated agreements with the top leaders. In 1972, this work resulted in Nixon visiting China and making a treaty with the Russians to limit nuclear weapons. Kissinger made mistakes, too, such as his involvement in the decision to bomb Cambodia in the early 1970s. His decisions have not always been popular or morally defensible, but he is inarguably a shrewd policymaker and brilliant thinker.

Betty Friedan

Betty Friedan was born Betty Naomi Goldstein. The daughter of Jewish immigrant parents who settled in Peoria, Illinois, Friedan watched as her father, a street-corner button peddler, struggled to survive, and her mother, a newspaper editor, was forced out of her job as soon as she married. A woman's place, it was believed, was in the home.

A brilliant student who graduated from college at the top of her class, Friedan followed her mother's lead into newspaper writing. After marrying Carl Friedan, she asked for leave to have a baby. She was fired and replaced by a man.

This led Friedan to years of study of what women really wanted in their lives—and why they couldn't have it. The result was her 1963 best-selling book *The Feminine Mystique*, questioning the role of women. Her exploration of the issue also led to the creation of NOW, the National Organization for Women. Friedan was founding president, and her first task was securing new laws that protected women's equal right to work.

Estée Lauder

Lauder, founder of the billion-dollar cosmetics company that bears her name, was born in Queens, New York, in 1908, the daughter of Hungarian immigrants. Like many immigrant children, Estée (named after an aunt in Hungary) at first turned her back on her parents' traditions. "I wanted to be 100 percent American," she remembers.

But it was a member of her family who shaped her life. Uncle John Shotz was a chemist who specialized in skin creams. "I watched as he created secret formulas that magically made your skin feel like spun silk," Lauder recalls. "I recognized in John my true path."

Working first in small beauty shops, Lauder learned how to make cosmetics and sell them, often by giving a free sample with every sale. But her real goal was placing her cosmetics in a New York City department store. One day that order came, which led to many more orders and, in time, an international business that sells cosmetics in seventy countries under famous brand names such as Clinique and Aramis.

Jonas Salk

In the early 1950s, a midsummer headache and stiff neck were known as the first signs of a crippling disease feared by every parent and child. The disease, poliomyelitis, struck more than 50,000 children each year, usually in the summer. More than 3,000 died from the illness during some years.

Credit the fact that you may never have heard of polio to Dr. Jonas Salk, developer of the first anti-polio vaccine. Salk was the son of a Jewish garment worker who stressed to his family the value of learning and education.

Salk learned that you could sometimes stop a disease by killing the virus that caused it and then injecting patients with the dead virus. This made the body produce antivirus chemicals that remained to fight the live virus should it appear. He wondered if this approach would work against polio. The danger was that if the virus was not completely dead, it might actually cause the disease. There was only one way to find out.

Against advice, Salk injected first himself, then his wife and his own children with "dead" polio virus. When the results were good, he sought more volunteers. During the mid-1950s, more than two million young "polio pioneers" took the injection. Later, an oral version was developed by Albert Sabin, another Jewish American doctor. Salk spent the rest of his life trying to find a way to fight other diseases. He died in 1994.

Barbra Streisand

Barbra (she dropped the second "a" so that "While there are many Barbaras, there's only one of me!") is one of the greatest entertainers of our time. She has starred in theater and film and produced many of her own works. The key to her talent is her magical singing voice and a personality that plays off her Brooklyn Jewish background. In *Funny Girl*, her first starring role, Streisand portrayed Fanny Brice, a Jewish comedienne. Even in superstardom, family has always been important. Streisand is close to her mother and misses even now the father who died when she was just fifteen months old. In a tribute to her dad, Streisand produced, directed, and starred in *Yentl*, a film about Jewish life in old Russia. She dedicated the film, and its theme song, "Papa, Can You Hear Me?", to the father she never knew.

Ruth Bader Ginsburg

Since the days of Moses, the Jews have been lawgivers. In almost every nation in which they've lived freely, there have been Jewish lawyers and judges. In the United States, distinguished Supreme Court Justices of Jewish descent have included Louis Brandeis, Felix Frankfurter, Arthur Goldberg, Benjamin Cardozo, and Abe Fortas. Ruth Bader Ginsburg joined the Court in 1993. Ginsburg is the second woman Justice, following Sandra Day O'Connor.

Ginsburg was born in Brooklyn in 1933 to a family of Russian Jewish immigrants. She graduated first in her class in public school, finished high school with honors and won a scholarship to Cornell University, then enrolled as one of only nine women in a class of 500 at Harvard Law School. Married in 1954 to Martin Ginsburg, she confidently set out for a career in law, only to find that most top firms had no interest in hiring women. She turned to teaching, and in time became a lawyer for groups seeking equal rights. She defended the causes of women and Native Americans, for example. In one case, she defended the right of a Jewish army officer to wear a yarmulke while on duty. In 1993, President Bill Clinton nominated her to the Supreme Court.

Steven Spielberg

Spielberg is one of the world's top filmmakers, the creator of *Jaws*, *E.T.*, and *Jurassic Park*. But the movie Spielberg is proudest of is *Schindler's List*, his personal tribute to the Jews of the Holocaust. His mother's family, of Russian immigrant stock, included an actor who performed Shakespeare in Yiddish.

Jerry Seinfeld

Growing up in Long Island, New York, comedian and actor Jerry Seinfeld says that he was not even the funniest member of his family. At the dinner table or other family gatherings, it was always Seinfeld's father who earned the most laughs. He demonstrated to Jerry the importance of humor in life. By the age of thirteen, Seinfeld had decided that his career would be in comedy. Not the most popular kid in school, Seinfeld watched a lot of television rather than hanging out with other kids. This provided him with inspiration for his career. He began to fine-tune his art, going so far as to tape interviews with his pet parakeet.

After graduating from Queens College in 1976 with degrees in theater and communication arts, Seinfeld set out immediately to achieve his career goals. The road to fame was rough. Seinfeld spent much of his early career working late nights at New York comedy clubs and taking part-time jobs to support himself. After five years of club appearances and a brief stint as a sitcom writer, Seinfeld got his break. His stand-up act on *The Tonight Show* in 1981 was a great success, earning him high-paying comedy appearances across the country.

In 1989, Seinfeld was asked by NBC to do a special. Seinfeld recruited his friend and fellow comedian Larry David to help him write the script. NBC liked the script so much that they wanted to make it into a TV comedy series. *Seinfeld* became one of the most popular programs on TV. Seinfeld has joined the long tradition of Jewish comedians, including Lenny Bruce, Henny Youngman, Milton Berle, Fanny Brice, Woody Allen, Gilda Radner, and George Burns.

Annie Leibovitz

The work of photographer Annie Leibovitz has appeared in magazines, advertisements, and museum exhibitions.

Leibovitz is known for her tenacity and patience, often spending hours sitting with her subjects or even moving in with them in pursuit of the perfect shot. Her perseverance pays off, however; her photos are said to cut through the false front of fame to reveal a vulnerability in her subjects never before captured on film. Aside from her work as a photographer, Leibovitz was also a member of the archaeological team that excavated King Solomon's temple in 1969.

Resources

JEWISH TRADITIONS AND LIFE

Dawidowicz, Lucy S., ed. *The Golden Tradition: Jewish Life and Thought in Eastern Europe.* **New York: Schocken Books, 1984.**

> Edited by one of America's best-known Jewish American historians, this work includes letters, autobiographies, and other documents from the sixteenth century to the Holocaust.

Dobroszycki, Lucjan, and Kirschenblatt-Gimblett, Barbara. *Image Before My Eyes: A Photographic History of Jewish Life in Poland.* **New York: Schocken Books, 1977.**

> A dazzling pictorial history. Photos come from the YIVO Institute, the leading authority on Jews in Eastern Europe.

Fleuk, Toby Knebel. *Passover as I Remember It.* **New York: Knopf, 1994.**

> Description of preparations for Passover in a small Polish village in the years before World War II. The village no longer exists.

Harris, Lis. *Holy Days: The World of a Hassidic Family.* **New York: Summit Books, 1985.**

> To outsiders, Hasidic Jews can be a mystery. In following one family's daily life, ceremonies, joys, and sorrows, Harris helps readers understand a people and a culture.

Helmreich, William. *World of the Yeshiva: An Intimate Portrait of Orthodox Judaism.* **Free Press/Macmillan, 1982.**

Helmreich enrolled in a yeshiva and wrote this book from personal experience. He also interviewed both teachers and students.

Mintl, Jerome R. *Legends of the Hassidim*. Chicago: University of Chicago Press, 1968.

More than 300 folktales that illustrate Hasidic life, thought, and history.

Patai, Raphael. *The Vanished World of Jewry*. New York: Macmillan, 1980.

A photo history of Judaism in eastern and central Europe, but also in rarely seen communities in North Africa and India.

Rosenberg, Roy A. *The Concise Guide to Judaism: History, Practice, Faith*. Munich, Germany: Mentor, 1990.

Ancient history, mysticism, philosophy, modern Judaism, the Jewish calendar, and a variety of other aspects of Judaism are covered in this clearly written guide.

Roskies, Diane K., and Roskies, David G. *The Shtetl Book*. New York: Ktav Publishing, 1979.

Meant as a school text, this book focuses on daily life and is peppered with actual documents, "you are there" descriptions, and stories from literary sources.

Salsitz, Norman. *A Jewish Boyhood in Poland*. Syracuse, New York: Syracuse University Press, 1992.

A description of life in the small town of Kolbusowa, Poland, before World War II.

Singer, Isaac Bashevis. *In My Father's Court*. New York: Farrar, Straus & Giroux, 1966.

Singer is one of the great Yiddish storytellers. In this work, he recalls the special Jewish religious court run by his father in their hometown. Such courts still exist today.

Zborowski, Mark, and Herzog, Elizabeth. *Life Is with People: The Culture of the Shtetl.* **New York: Schocken Books, 1962.**

A view of small-town life in eastern Europe. Includes interviews with former shtetl dwellers.

THE JEWISH AMERICAN EXPERIENCE

Angel, Marc D. *La America: The Sephardic Experience in the United States.* **Philadelphia: Jewish Publication Service, 1982.**

Details the experience of Sephardic Jews from Turkey, Syria, and Bulgaria in the United States between 1899 and 1925, including their failed efforts to form a Sephardic cultural organization.

Berkow, Ira. *Survival in a Bazaar.* **Garden City, New York: Doubleday, 1977.**

The story of the famous Maxwell Street shopping area in Chicago and its Jewish creators.

Birmingham, Stephen. *The Grandees.* **New York: Harper and Row, 1971.**

According to the author, the New York Sephardic community considered itself the "nobility of Jewry." You'll meet the leading families and learn what they thought of the "pushy Germans" who followed them to America. Includes a unique genealogical chart of important families.

———. *Our Crowd.* **New York: Berkeley Books, 1985.**

Recalls the Guggenheims, Loebs, Belmonts, and other members of Jewish "high society."

Birstein, Ann. *The Rabbi on 47th Street.* **New York: Dial Press, 1982.**

The author's father was the spiritual leader of a New York synagogue known as "the Actors' Temple," in that it catered to stars of the entertainment business. Behind-the-scenes stories of the faith of Eddie Cantor, Red Buttons, Sophie Tucker, and others.

Cohen, Naomi W. *Encounter with Emancipation: German Jews in the United States, 1830–1914.* **Philadelphia: Jewish Publication Society, 1985.**

Focusing on the first major Jewish immigrant group, the German Jews, the author writes about business, culture, politics, and the struggle to be German, Jewish, and American all at once.

Eisen, Arnold M. *The Chosen People in America.* **Bloomington: Indiana University Press, 1983.**

Can the "Chosen People" keep their uniqueness and at the same time become "American"? Eisen explores this question and how the various branches of Judaism have handled the issue.

Feingold, Harry L. *Zion in America: The Jewish Experience from Colonial Times to the Present.* **New York: Hippocrene Books, 1981.**

This work moves quickly through the decades, covering large themes rather than detail. The author discusses how American Jews have kept their identity and compares the opportunities Jews had in the United States as compared to other nations.

Frommer, Myrna Katz. *It Happened in the Catskills.* **San Diego: Harcourt, Brace and Jovanovich, 1991.**

Revisit the period during the 1940s and 1950s when the Catskill Mountain resorts were a center of Jewish society each summer.

Harris, Leon A. *Merchant Princes: Jewish Families Who Built Great Department Stores.* **New York: Harper & Row, 1979.**

How Macy's, Gimbels, Abraham & Straus, and other great stores started out and became some of the largest American businesses.

Howe, Irving, ed. *World of Our Fathers.* **New York: Simon & Schuster, 1989.**

Account of the migration of Eastern European Jews to the United States, and especially to New York City. Howe explores the bustling streets, daily life, businesses, schools and synagogues, artists, and writers.

Joselit, Jenna Weissman. *Our Gang: Jewish Crime and the New York Jewish Community, 1900–1940.* **Bloomington: Indiana University Press, 1983.**

Weissman introduces you to Jewish tough guys, hit men, and con men; she tells how they preyed on Jew and non-Jew alike; covers how the community fought back; and explains how gang members used crime as a path to middle-class life.

———. *The Wonders of America.* **New York: Hill and Wang, 1994.**

Though this book covers American Jewish history from 1880 to 1950, much of it details the "next generation" Jews who moved their parents' dreams to the next level of American society.

Kanfer, Stefan. *A Summer World.* **New York: Farrar, Straus & Giroux, 1989.**

Called the Jewish Alps and the Borscht Belt, New York State's Catskill Mountains region was the summer playground for many immigrant families.

Karp, Abraham J. *Haven and Home: A History of the Jews in America.* **New York: Schocken Books, 1985.**

Surveys the history of American Jews from 1654 to the present, emphasizing the social and cultural differences in the various communities.

Libo, Kenneth, and Howe, Irving. *We Lived There Too*. New York: Marek/St. Martin's Press, 1984.

Similar to Howe's book *World of Our Fathers*, this volume includes many original documents and has a lively style. But it extends the history of the immigrants beyond the big cities and into the American heartland.

Lobas, Vladimir. *Taxi from Hell: Confessions of a Russian Hack*. New York: Soho Press, Inc., 1991.

Although humorously written, this book explores the difficulties of language and adaptation confronting the latest wave of Jewish immigrants to the United States.

Marinbach, Bernard. *Galveston: Ellis Island of the West*. Albany: State University of New York Press, 1993.

From 1907 to 1914, this Texas city was the gateway for many families now living in the Southwest.

Meckler, Brenda Weisberg. *Papa Was a Farmer*. Chapel Hill, NC: Algonquin Books of Chapel Hill, 1988.

The story of a Jewish farm family in Ohio in the 1900s.

Meltzer, Milton, ed. *The Jewish Americans: A History in their Own Words*. New York: Crowell, 1982.

Accounts of personal experiences taken from letters, journals, diaries, speeches, and autobiographies.

Metzker, Isaac, ed. *A Bintel Brief: Sixty Years of Letters from the Lower East Side to the Jewish Daily Forward*. New York: Behrman House, 1982.

A *Bintel Brief* was an advice column in the Yiddish-language newspaper that served the Lower East Side, a kind of Yiddish *Dear Abby*.

Orlove, Benjamin S. *In My Father's Study*. Iowa City: University of Iowa Press, 1995.

A fond remembrance of life in a Jewish home in the early part of the twentieth century. Concentrates on one family's customs.

Pogrebin, Letty Cottin. *Deborah, Golda, and Me: Being Female and Jewish in America*. New York: Crown, 1991.

The founder of *Ms.* magazine grapples with her identity as a feminist and a Jew. She seeks female role models in the Bible and examines topics—such as Israel and the Palestinian question—through a feminist lens.

Rischin, Moses. *The Promised City: New York's Jews, 1870–1914*. Cambridge, MA: Harvard University Press, 1977.

This landmark work was one of the first to explore the rapid changes Jews underwent in moving from Europe to the United States. Rischin argues that the speed of the change was a key factor in how Jewish American life later developed. Details the development of the Lower East Side from 1870 to 1914, highlighting the transition from German to Russian immigrants, and the role of the *Landsmannshaft* groups.

Rochlin, Harriet, and Rochlin, Fred. *Pioneer Jews: A New Life in the American West*. Boston: Houghton-Mifflin, 1984.

Explores the travels, businesses, and lifestyles of Jews in the West of the 1800s.

Rosten, Leo. *The Education of H*y*m*a*n K*a*p*l*a*n*. New York: Harcourt Brace Jovanovich, 1968.

As a Jewish immigrant trying to learn the language, the fictional Hyman exemplifies the struggle many real-life Jews faced and the energy and sense of humor that helped them succeed.

Sachs, Marilyn. *Call Me Ruth*. **Garden City, NY: Doubleday, 1982.**

The story of the union movement in a novel of a young girl who fears her mother's involvement with radical organizers will end in disaster for them both.

Schooner, Allon, comp. *Portal to America: The Lower East Side, 1870–1925*. **New York: Holt, Rinehart & Winston, 1967.**

Views life on the Lower East Side through materials gathered for a major exhibit on the topic by New York's Jewish Museum.

Shapiro, Michael. *The Jewish 100*. **New York: Citadel Press, 1994.**

Shapiro ranks the Jews whose influence was greatest upon Jewish and world history. Includes a one-page or two-page biography on each of these pioneers in music, science, sports, literature, religion, philosophy, and diplomacy.

Simon, Kate. *Bronx Primitive: Portraits in a Childhood*. **New York: Viking Press, 1982.**

Immigrant families moved from the Lower East Side to better neighborhoods in New York's outer boroughs. Read about what life was like in the Bronx.

Simons, Howard. *Jewish Times*. **Boston: Houghton-Mifflin, 1988.**

Personal statements about the American Jewish experience. Prominent Jews (for example, TV interviewer Larry King) tell about growing up in various parts of the United States.

FILMS

The Chosen, **1981. Directed by Jeremy Paul Kagan.**

An adaptation a Chaim Potok novel depicting a friendship between a young Hasidic student and an Americanized Jewish boy in Brooklyn in the 1940s.

Crossing Delancey, 1982. Directed by Joan Micklin Silver.

Generations clash as a traditional Jewish *bubbe* (grandmother) tries to make a marriage match for her thoroughly modern granddaughter.

Fiddler on the Roof, 1971. Directed by Norman Jewison.

Based on the folktales of Shalom Aleichem, this is the story of Tevye, a poor milkman, and his wife and five daughters living in the Pale of Russia at the turn of the century.

Funny Girl, 1968. Directed by William Wyler. *Funny Lady*, 1975. Directed by Herbert Ross.

These films, adapted from a hit Broadway show, tell the life story of Fanny Brice, a Jewish entertainer from Brooklyn who became a Broadway star in the 1920s.

Gentlemen's Agreement, 1947. Directed by Elia Kazan.

A non-Jewish reporter covers a story about how a secret agreement keeps Jews out of certain jobs and social clubs.

Hester Street, 1975. Directed by Joan Micklin Silver.

The grittier side of the immigrant life is told in a sensitive portrayal of a shy young immigrant woman, who must deal with the pressures of life in a new and unfamiliar world.

The Jazz Singer, 1927, 1980. Directed by Alan Crosland (1927) and Richard Fleischer (1980).

Explores the struggle between generations in a new land. The first film starred Al Jolson; the second, Neil Diamond.

Yentl, 1983. Directed by Barbra Streisand.

Based on a story by Isaac Bashevis Singer. Yentl is a young Jewish woman in Poland who won't accept the notion that she can't attend yeshiva like the men.

Chapter 5
Never Forget, Never Again

Nothing in their 4,000-year history could prepare European Jews for what awaited them in the twentieth century.

First World War I and then the Russian Revolution shut down migration within Europe and from Europe to the United States. Then new laws were passed, closing the "Golden Door" to the United States. Only those with immediate family already in the States could still enter freely.

For those trapped in Russia, the situation was grim. The Communists had taken over. They battled among themselves, and each new leadership that took power sought to eliminate anyone who did not agree with them. Thousands of Jews were slaughtered in the civil war and in the plots and acts of revenge that took place.

In 1929, Europe and the United States were wracked by economic depression. Long-established businesses failed, and jobs disappeared in record numbers. For the first time in their lives, many in the middle class understood what it was like to be poor. The poor became beggars in the streets.

The various nations reacted in different ways to these troubles. The United States offered its citizens social programs and government-sponsored work. The Germans turned to the Nazis, a small political group that seemed to come out of nowhere and took over Germany in a legal election. They did it by promising the voters to restore their nation's military greatness after its defeat in World War I, and by promising jobs. On the basis of these promises, Nazi Party leader Adolf Hitler became chancellor of Germany in 1933.

There was another facet of the Nazis' program: They blamed Germany's troubles—and the world's—on the Jews.

American Jews and recent Jewish immigrants expressed their solidarity with the plight of their fellow Jews in Europe during World War II. In 1938, Jewish merchants in the Bronx closed their stores for one hour in protest against anti-Semitism in Germany.

Hitler claimed that Jews worldwide had planned World War I and the economic troubles to line their pockets with profit. He stated his belief that Jews were an inferior race that "polluted" European society. Hitler made it very clear that he would rid Europe of these "vermin" once and for all. In 1941, Hitler promised a "final solution" to the "Jewish problem." This "final solution" was the infamous concentration camps and extermination squads that killed millions of Jews.

Frightened Jewish women and children in Warsaw are led out of their homes by Nazi soldiers during the German siege of Warsaw in 1943. This photo was presented at the Nazi war crimes trials in Nuremburg, Germany, as evidence of Nazi atrocities.

Killing Factories

In the past, others had wanted to eliminate the Jews, but the Nazis had something new—twentieth-century science and technology. They also had the will to use it.

During World War II, a chain of death camps was built. Each was a killing factory capable of wiping out thousands of Jews each day. Its victims were stripped of their clothes, jewelry, eyeglasses, hair, and gold teeth, which the Nazis collected for later sale. The names of these camps—Auschwitz, Treblinka, Bergen-Belsen, Dachau, and others—will forever haunt Jewish memories and those of non-Jews as well.

When the war began, German armies swept across Europe. Wherever they went, a special killing force called the *Einsatzgruppen* followed. Jews were rounded up and forced to live in ghettos, if they didn't already. That made it easy for German troopers to jam them into freight trains and ship them to the camps.

A Jewish boy is forced by German soldiers to cut his father's beard in 1933, the first year of the Holocaust—a period of systematic persecution and attempted genocide of European Jews by Adolf Hitler's Nazis.

Many have wondered why the Jews, who outnumbered their guards, did not fight back or escape to the forests and mountains. One reason is that they were falsely told they were being "resettled" in peaceful areas. But Nobel Prize-winning author and death camp survivor Elie Wiesel offers another explanation. It was because they had been promised that wherever they were going, their families would stay together. "Family unity is one of our most important traditions," writes Wiesel. "The Nazis knew that and used it to murder us."

The Nazi persecution of the Jews lasted twelve years, from 1933, when Hitler took power, to 1945, the end of the war. Other people, such as Gypsies and homosexuals, were also slaughtered by the Nazis during the Holocaust, but the Jews in particular were targeted. Six million Jews—mostly women, children, and the weak and old—were brutally killed. The world Jewish population went from 16 million down to 10 million. The Holocaust remains an evil beyond understanding, but never, the civilized world hopes, beyond remembering.

Following the war, relief organizations helped the surviving European Jews to rebuild their lives, wherever they wanted to be. Many were "displaced persons," with no home or family left in Europe.

Some of these refugees remained in Europe. More than 100,000 entered the United States. Still others settled in the new state of Israel.

It is likely that if members of your family arrived in the United States from Europe in the late 1940s or early 1950s, they are survivors of the Holocaust. Those who survived the camps often bear numbers tattooed on an arm. But everyone who lived through the horror is marked in some way—physically or emotionally.

The effect on Europe's Jews was staggering. Some 80 percent of the world's Jews lived in Europe at the start of World War II. Only 30 percent lived there at war's end. Few European Jewish families escaped some effect from the Holocaust. One survivor lost thirty-eight family members at the Auschwitz death camp.

Resources

THE HOLOCAUST AND ANTI-SEMITISM

Berenbaum, Michael. *The World Must Know.* **Boston: Little, Brown, 1993.**

Written as part of the United States Holocaust Museum opening, this dramatic work includes many photos from the museum, as well as accompanying text.

Das Pres, Terrance. *The Survivor: An Anatomy of Life in the Death Camps.* **Oxford: Oxford University Press, 1976.**

Examines the specific human qualities that allowed some victims to find the strength to survive the disaster and at the same time maintain their dignity as humans and as Jews.

Dawidowicz, Lucy S. *The War Against the Jews, 1933–1945.* **New York: Bantam Books, 1976.**

Many call this the best book for general reading on the Holocaust. An appendix gives a nation-by-nation account of the fate of European Jews.

Dinnerstein, Leonard. *Anti-Semitism in America.* **London: Oxford University Press, 1994.**

Discrimination against Jews was not confined to Europe. The author explores the reasons, methods, publications, and personalities behind anti-Jewish hatred in the United States since the 1790s.

Dobroszycki, Lucjan, ed. *Chronicle of the Lodz Ghetto.* **New Haven: Yale University Press, 1984.**

You can get a sense for what life was like under Nazi control in this harrowing record of simple day-to-day events. Officials recorded each day's weather, births, and marriages—and its suicides, shootings, and shipments to the death camps. The editor himself lived in the ghetto.

Eisenberg, Azriel, ed. *The Lost Generation: Children in the Holocaust.* **New York: Pilgrim Press, 1982.**

How did children react to the horrors of the time? Eisenberg has put together 100 accounts by those who were there. It's painful reading, but a way to see how young eyes perceived these evil acts.

Eliach, Yaffa. *Hasidic Tales of the Holocaust.* **London: Oxford University Press, 1982.**

Hasidic Jews are known for an optimistic view of life. The collector of these true stories, often told as folktales, reveals that a powerful internal faith sustained them in the Holocaust.

Epstein, Helen. *Children of the Holocaust: Conversations with Sons and Daughters of Survivors.* **New York: Bantam Books, 1960.**

Epstein, whose parents survived Auschwitz, has interviewed other children of survivors and found they all had problems dealing with the horrors their parents faced.

Fein, Helen. *Accounting for Genocide.* **Chicago: University of Chicago Press, 1979.**

A study of how citizens and local officials of each nation reacted to the war against the Jews, and how these differing attitudes and reactions were a major reason many died—or lived.

Ferencz, Benjamin. *Less Than Slaves.* **Cambridge, MA: Harvard University Press, 1979.**

An account of slave labor in war factories during the Holocaust and the terrible conditions these workers faced.

Fleming, Gerald. *Hitler and the Final Solution.* **Berkeley: University of California Press, 1984.**

Some people now claim that the Holocaust was not as bad as reported, and even that Hitler never ordered it. Through interviews and documents, Fleming offers proof of the full scope of the disaster and that it was indeed ordered personally by the Nazi leader.

Frank, Anne. *Diary of a Young Girl*. New York: Doubleday, 1995.

Perhaps the best-known individual caught in the Holocaust, Frank was a teenager in Holland when the Nazis marched through. Her family hid in an attic, where she kept an amazing diary that shows how hope can live in the worst of worlds.

Greene, Bette. *Summer of My German Soldier*. New York: Dial Books, 1973.

A classic young-adult novel about a young Jewish girl in Arkansas who befriends an escaped German prisoner of war. She battles an abusive father and the racism in her community.

Gutman, Israel. *Resistance: The Warsaw Ghetto Uprising*. Boston: Houghton Mifflin, 1994.

Gutman, a survivor of three Nazi concentration camps, recalls the events of the Jewish revolt in Warsaw on April 19, 1943. Published in association with the Holocaust Memorial Museum in Washington, DC.

Hay, Malcolm V. *Europe and the Jews*. New York: Freedom Library Press, 1981.

Details more than 1,900 years of anti-Semitism, including such falsehoods as "ritual murder." Also discusses Jewish stereotypes from the Middle Ages through the Nazi period.

Hersey, John. *The Wall*. New York: Knopf, 1950.

This classic work is in the form of a diary of people living in the Warsaw ghetto in Poland in the days leading up to their forced evacuation to the death camps.

Jacobson, Ken. *Embattled Selves: Jewish Identity and the Holocaust.* **New York: Atlantic Monthly Press, 1994.**

Twenty-four survivors of the Holocaust discuss how they dealt with their Jewishness during World War II, attempting to reach conclusions about the nature of human identity.

Kaplan, Chaim A. *The Warsaw Diary of Chaim A. Kaplan.* **New York: Macmillan, 1981.**

Kaplan, the principal of a Hebrew school, died at the Treblinka Camp. This is his account of the day-to-day happenings in the ghetto.

Keller, Ulrich, ed. *The Warsaw Ghetto in Photographs: 206 Views Made in 1941.* **New York: Dover, 1984.**

Taken by German photographers, this remarkable collection shows street activity, local officials, entertainment, and children at play.

Keneally, Thomas. *Schindler's List.* **New York: Penguin, 1983.**

The basis for a 1993 Academy Award-winning motion picture, this book tells the story of a German factory manager, Oskar Schindler, who outwardly cooperated with the Nazis while secretly saving the lives of more than 1,000 Jews.

Korczak, Janus. *Ghetto Diary.* **New York: Schocken Books, 1978.**

The author, head of a ghetto orphanage, had the chance to save his own life but would not leave his children. All died together.

Lester, Elegnore. *Wallenberg: The Man in the Iron Web.* **New York: Prentice-Hall, 1982.**

Raoul Wallenberg, a Swedish diplomat, used his protected status to save tens of thousands of Hungarian Jews. He disappeared at war's end, some say shot as a spy by the Russians.

Lewis, Bernard. *Semites and Anti-Semites: An Inquiry into Conflict and Prejudice*. New York: Norton, 1986.

Lewis examines anti-Semitism throughout history, focusing in particular on its effects on religion, history, and psychology. He examines anti-Semitism as both a political policy and personal bias.

Litvinoff, Barry. *The Burning Bush*. New York: E. P. Dutton, 1988.

The history of anti-Semitism, including lies about Jews, physical attacks, and progress made in combatting this form of hate.

Marrus, Michael, and Paxton, Robert O. *Vichy France and the Jews*. New York: Schocken Books, 1981.

Details how, after the fall of France in 1940, some French leaders set up a German-controlled puppet government in the city of Vichy, which actively helped the Nazis find and kill thousands of Jews.

Suhl, Yuri, ed. *They Fought Back: The Story of the Jewish Resistance in Nazi Europe*. New York: Schocken Books, 1975.

Suhl has gathered proof that there was resistance in almost every ghetto and camp. The book is well written, and the stories are inspiring.

Uris, Leon. *Mila 18*. Garden City, NY: Doubleday, 1961.

The story of the Warsaw Ghetto uprising, in which lightly armed Jews faced down German tanks and field guns, teaching the world a lesson about Jewish courage.

Weiss, Peter. *The Investigation.* **New York: Atheneum, 1966.**

Actual testimony from the war crimes trials of a number of high-ranking Nazi officials.

Wiesel, Elie. *Legends of Our Time.* **New York: Schocken Books, 1968.**

Wiesel tells his own story as a Holocaust survivor and shares his memories of friends and teachers.

————. *Night/Dawn/Day.* **New York: Aronson, 1985.**

Actually three works in one. *Night* is Wiesel's memory of life in the death camp; the other books tell of the lives of survivors after the war. The books are also available separately.

Yahil, Leni. *The Rescue of Danish Jewry: Test of a Democracy.* **Philadelphia: Jewish Publication Society, 1983.**

Of all the governments under German control, Denmark's was the only one to refuse to help destroy its Jewish citizens, and the Nazis backed down.

FILMS

Anne Frank Remembered, **1995. Directed by Jon Blair.**

Winner of the Oscar for Best Documentary, this film features interviews with eyewitnesses who knew Anne Frank and shows us the reconstructed rooms where she and her family lived.

The Diary of Anne Frank, **1959. Directed by George Stevens.**

The film version of the book (see above) tells the story in a touching and understated way.

Europa, Europa, **1991. Directed by Agnieszka Holland.**

A humor-laced drama about a German Jewish boy who,

while trying to escape the Nazis, is mistakenly drafted into Hitler's army. The film is based on a true story.

The Nasty Girl, 1990. Directed by Michael Verhoeven.

A young German woman discovers the truth about her hometown during the Nazi period.

Schindler's List, 1993. Directed by Steven Spielberg.

Adapted from the book, and shot in black and white like a 1940s newsreel, Steven Spielberg's film paints a picture of the horrors of the Holocaust, but it also carries the message that mercy and good will defeat evil.

Shoah, 1985. Directed by Claude Lanzmann.

A nine-hour, two-part documentary about the Holocaust. In-depth interviews with Holocaust survivors—including Jews, non-Jews, even former Nazis—provide a detailed examination of the events, allowing viewers to form their own responses.

Sophie's Choice, 1982. Directed by Alan J. Pakula.

The stormy relationship between a Polish Catholic woman and a Jewish man, as observed by the Southerner who shares their home. A link is drawn between the couple's relationship and the Nazi persecution of the Jews. Based on the novel by William Styron. For mature audiences.

Voyage of the Damned, 1976. Directed by Stuart Rosenberg.

The true story of the S.S. *St. Louis*, which sailed for Cuba and then the United States just before the outset of World War II, carrying 900 Jews seeking refuge from the Nazis. The ship reached its destination, only to be turned back. Most of the passengers were later arrested and died in the camps.

Chapter 6
Two Promised Lands

There is an old Jewish saying that "Whenever God closes a window, He opens a door." The door that opened after the Holocaust was one the Jews had been hoping would open for nearly 2,000 years. It was the birth of the new Jewish state of Israel.

Even after the historical departure of most Jews from Israel, a few Jews still lived in the area alongside large Arab populations. But in Europe in the late 1800s a movement was begun among some Jews to return to the land of their ancestors. In an 1896 book, *The Jewish State*, Jewish Austrian journalist Theodor Herzl proposed a remedy to the problem of anti-Semitism, which was on the rise in Europe. Herzl suggested that the creation of a Jewish state would provide a safe haven for European Jews from the dangers of pogroms and other acts of anti-Semitism. Those who adopted Herzl's view were called Zionists, for their desire to return to Zion, an ancient name for Israel. In 1897, Herzl organized the first Zionist Congress with the aim of establishing a home for the Jews in the land of their ancestors.

At the time the area now known as Israel was officially known as Palestine and was controlled by the Turks. In 1917 the land was taken by Great Britain, and in the same year, in the Balfour Declaration, the British pledged that they would support the establishment of a Jewish homeland in Palestine. In 1920, a British Mandate was formally recognized. However, despite the Balfour Declaration and owing in part to strong Arab pressure, Britain did little to aid the Zionist cause. The British continued to oversee Palestine until 1948. Between 1920 and 1948, the Jewish population in Palestine grew from 50,000 to 600,000, largely as a result of refugees fleeing the Nazis. Simultaneously, Arabs from Syria and Lebanon immigrated to the same area.

After the horror of the Holocaust, the Jews' desire for a homeland could no longer be refused. In 1947, the United Nations General Assembly voted to partition Palestine into an Arab and a Jewish state. The Arabs rejected partition. Under increasing pressure from Arabs and Jews, both of whom wanted to control the land, the British relinquished their mandate over Palestine in May 1948. On May 14 of that year, the state of Israel was established by a United Nations declaration. Large numbers of Palestinians became refugees and exiles after the creation of the state of Israel.

Palestinian Arabs, afraid of losing their land, rejected the UN declaration. Supported by Arab forces from Jordan, Iraq, Lebanon, and Syria, Palestinians attacked the newborn Israeli state. The fighting continued through January 1949, but the Israelis successfully beat back the Arab invasion. Arab-Israeli conflicts have since erupted in 1956, 1967, 1973, and 1982.

In the mid-1990s, great strides were made toward establishing peace between Israel and its neighbors. Israel signed peace agreements with both Egypt and Jordan. In 1993 and 1995, Yasser Arafat, leader of the Palestine Liberation Organization (PLO), and Yitzhak Rabin, Prime Minister of Israel, signed peace accords between their peoples. In the accords, Israel agreed to yield control of certain areas of Israel to Palestinian self-rule in exchange for peace. But just days after he signed the second peace accord with Arafat, Rabin was assassinated by an Israeli opposed to the peace process. Clearly, the issue of who owns the land is still a sensitive one for Palestinians and Israelis alike.

It is possible that members of your family now reside in modern Israel. Several hundred thousand European Jews found refuge there after the war, and many American Jews have moved to Israel to live in the land of their biblical ancestors. Under its Law of Return, Israel allows any Jew of good character to enter and become a citizen.

Yafim and Masha Mazin, Russian Jews who immigrated to the United States in 1988, participate in a special marriage ceremony in West Orange, New Jersey, with five other Russian Jewish couples. The couples had been married in civil ceremonies in the Soviet Union, where traditional Jewish rites were forbidden.

If you could follow the roots of your family tree to its very earliest beginnings, those beginnings would be in Israel. The Law of Return means that, if you wish, your family's future can be there too.

The New Jewish Immigrants

Meanwhile, the United States has sometimes been viewed as a "promised land" for Jews living under conditions of political and religious oppression. In the late 1980s and 1990s, major economic problems in Russia and continued anti-Semitism created a new wave of Jewish immigrants. More than 50,000 Russian Jews have made their way to the United States. Many have settled in the borough of Brooklyn in New York City.

The pattern these recent immigrants follow is much like that of the earlier waves. Russian Jews have set up synagogues, schools, and their own newspapers. When necessary, they take jobs at the bottom of the ladder of success, working as waiters and cabdrivers, and looking forward to greater opportunity in the future. Others, with greater skills, have forged successful professional careers in their adopted country.

Like other émigrés, they have problems with crime, with learning English, with keeping their identity and their faith while becoming Americans. But they have a wonderful chance for success.

Jewish émigrés from the former Soviet Union have a special challenge in that many must rediscover Jewish traditions after immigrating to the United States. The Soviet regime did not officially permit the practice of religion. While some synagogues did remain open, it was primarily elderly Jewish citizens who attended them. Thus, some Jews who grew up in the Soviet Union had never been to a synagogue, never celebrated a Passover seder or a bar mitzvah. While these Jewish immigrants do not always consider themselves religious, some take the newfound opportunity to embrace their religion and learn more about the traditions their parents and grandparents were not permitted to pass on. Some send their children to religious schools so their children receive the religious education they never had. They demonstrate the commitment to their faith and the resiliency that has distinguished the Jewish people for centuries.

Resources

Begin, Menachem. *The Revolt.* **New York: Dell, 1978.**

Begin fought in the war for the creation of the State of Israel and years later served as its prime minister. This is a personal view of his younger years.

Collins, Larry, and Lapierre, Dominique. *O Jerusalem!* **New York: Pocket Books, 1973.**

Before the state of Israel was declared, Jews on the scene often fought against the British then in control of the area. This is the story of those actions and how they affected the Jews, the British, and the Arabs living in the region.

Gerner, Deborah J. *One Land, Two Peoples: The Conflict Over Palestine.* **Boulder, CO: Westview Press, 1991.**

Historical analysis of the tension between Jews and Palestinians in Jerusalem, with discussion of Arab-Israeli conflicts.

Grose, Peter. *Israel in the Mind of America.* **New York: Knopf, 1983.**

How did Americans, Jews and non-Jews alike, feel about the creation of a new Israel? The author explains how those feelings changed from the 1800s on.

Herzl, Theodor. *The Jewish State.* **New York: Herzl Press, 1970.**

Called the father of modern Israel, Herzl sets forth his belief that the Jews should not give up their identity and join another culture, but instead should return to their biblical homeland.

Lilker, Shalom. *Kibbutz Judaism: A New Tradition in the Making.* **New York: Cornwall Books, 1982.**

A kibbutz is an experiment in living together, in which a group shares space, food, successes, and failures. Lilker explains how Jewish tradition is reflected in the kibbutz concept.

Marton, Kati. *A Death in Jerusalem.* **New York: Pantheon Books, 1994.**

Detailed account of the diplomatic history of the Israel-Arab War. Also explores the historical problem of terrorism in Jerusalem and throughout Israel.

Meir, Golda. *My Life.* **New York: Dell, 1975.**

As prime minister of Israel from 1969 to 1974, Meir was one of the first women to serve as a head of state. In this autobiography, she traces her life from her days of fighting in the war for independence to her position as leader of her nation.

Mozeson, Isaac, and Stavsky, Lois. *Jerusalem Mosaic: Young Voices from the Holy City.* **New York: Four Winds Press, 1994.**

An interesting look at Jewish-Arab relations through the eyes of Jerusalem's youth. Contains interviews with both Jewish and Palestinian young people.

Oppenheim, Carolyn Toll, ed. *Listening to American Jews: Sh'ma 1970–1987.* **New York: Adama Books, 1987.**

Collection of writings by Jews covering Judaism in the United States, the Jewish Diaspora, and attitudes of American Jews toward Israel.

Penkower, Monty Noam. *The Holocaust and Israel Reborn: From Catastrophe to Sovereignty.* **Urbana: University of Illinois Press, 1994.**

The history of the Jewish people from World War II through today. Topics covered are: the Holocaust, Zionism, and United States-Israeli relations.

Romann, Michael, and Weingrod, Alex. *Living Together Separately: Arabs and Jews in Contemporary Jerusalem.* **Princeton, NJ: Princeton University Press, 1991.**

Explores the fragile relationship between the Arabs and the Jews in Jerusalem, from the turn of the century through today.

Sacks, Jonathan, Rabbi. *One People?: Tradition, Modernity, and Jewish Unity.* **Washington, DC: B'nai B'rith Book Service, 1993.**

Explains in detail the complex relationship between secular and religious Jews in Israel, the United States, and throughout the world.

Shazar, Rachel K., ed. *The Plough Woman: Memoirs of the Pioneer Women of Palestine.* **Herzl Press, 1975.**

Personal accounts of fifty women who lived in Palestine in the early twentieth century of the hardships they faced, family concerns, and their attempts to create a society in which opportunities were equally open to women and men.

Shteiner, Puah. *Forever My Jerusalem: A Personal Account of the Siege and Surrender of Old Jerusalem's Old City in 1948.* **New York: Feldheim Publishers, 1987.**

Shteiner recounts the events of the 1948 siege of Jerusalem, when Palestinian Arab forces were joined by troops from Iraq, Lebanon, and Syria in an attack on Jewish forces in Israel.

Sinclair, Andrew. *Jerusalem: The Endless Crusade.* **New York: Crown Publishers, 1995.**

Discusses the historical and present-day importance of the city of Jerusalem to the religions of Judaism, Christianity, and Islam.

Uris, Leon. *Exodus*. Garden City, NY: Doubleday, 1958.

A story of Israeli resistance fighters who overcame the British blockade of Palestine to fight for the establishment of the Israeli state. A film version, starring Paul Newman, was made from the book.

Waskow, Arthur I. *These Holy Sparks: The Rebirth of the Jewish People*. San Fransisco: Harper & Row, 1983.

Explores the strength and perseverance of the Jewish people in both Israel and the United States, despite the challenges they have faced.

Chapter 7
Genealogical Ground Rules

Before you set out on your voyage into the past, you should be familiar with the rules of the road. They've been developed over years by people of many religions and nationalities seeking their pasts.

Work from the Known to the Unknown

Studying genealogy has been likened to crossing a bridge from the present to the past. It's a good comparison, especially when you think of it as an old bridge to an unknown destination, with weak spots in the planking. In such a situation, you'd walk carefully, testing each step.

Do the same in your research. If you're certain of a relative's position in your family history, seek to identify the next relative in the chain, not those two or three generations back. If you know for certain where forebears lived, seek their previous location next, not the city or town before that. Make each step a small one. Together, they'll form a road that will take you in the right direction. Even if you are interested primarily in learning about your ancestors who lived in Russia, for example, it is important not to "jump" to Russia without first having traced the path of your family from Russia to the United States.

Deal First with Memories

Historical information is like a river: The whole body of water flows away from you with each passing day, but some currents move faster than others. The kind that move away most quickly are human memories. If you don't get to written records or physical items right now, they'll likely still be there when you do get to them. That's not the case with memory.

It is common sense to interview relatives before you delve into any other kind of research. Interview the oldest relatives first, especially your great-grandparents, grandparents, and others of their age group. They will have the greatest range of experiences to tell you about. And they are most likely to have been personally touched by the great historical changes that have shaped Jewish history.

Confirm Your Facts

Depending on people's memories carries special problems. For one thing, memory fades with time. For another, people often remember the good and forget the bad. Or they may remember the good as better than it was, or the bad as worse. It's common for older people, for example, to recall that automobile makers no longer "make them as good as they used to," even though today's cars perform better in every way. Some who lived in crime-ridden parts of large cities point with pride to how they "survived." But at the time they lived there, the areas were tree-lined middle-class neighborhoods.

It's also human nature sometimes to retell one's role as more important than it actually was. Army supply clerks have become Medal of Honor winners in the retelling. And among Jewish families, "a cast of thousands," according to a leading genealogist, claim to be descended from famous rabbis and other famous figures.

That's why genealogists recommend that you confirm each key fact of your family's history with at least two sources. You might have a story told by a relative confirmed by a document, or by the story of another relative not in direct contact with the first. For example, you should still try to obtain a copy of your great-aunt's marriage certificate even if she has told you when she was married.

Should you join any of the major genealogical organizations, they'll demand such proof before recognizing your story as authentic, but it's good practice to get such confirmations even if your study is meant only for your own purposes.

A Jewish American Photo Album

Areas with heavy Jewish emigration 1882–present.

The long history of the Jewish people is a history of struggle against persecution, violence, and discrimination, as well as one of bravery, triumph, strength, and brilliant achievement. In the effort to sustain themselves against sometimes hostile circumstances, Jews migrated to many regions over many centuries, a phenomenon known as the Jewish Diaspora. The diverse geographical spread of Jewish migration will make your genealogical search challenging, but all the more fascinating. The Jewish holidays and customs in which you may participate with your family are traditions your ancestors brought with them as they traveled, even if they were not officially permitted to practice their religion. You may choose to explore your Jewish heritage by learning about Israel, perhaps even planning a visit there someday to see the landmarks and monuments that speak of the history of your people. But you don't have to travel to Israel to see the remarkable contributions of your forebears. The Jewish presence in the United States dates as early as 1654. Jewish Americans have helped shape American history by applying the lessons of their own past to other struggles for freedom and equality, such as the Civil Rights movement and the women's movement. Jewish Americans have successfully applied their skills and talents in every field imaginable.

The city of Jerusalem, located in central Israel between the Mediterranean Sea and the Dead Sea, is one of the most important sites in Jewish history. Once the capital of the Jewish kingdom under the rule of King David, Jerusalem again stands as the official capital of modern-day Israel.

U.S. presidents have historically played a significant role in the Middle East peace process. Israel is an important U.S. ally in the region for strategic and political reasons. Above, as President Bill Clinton looks on, the late Israeli Prime Minister Yitzhak Rabin (left) and Yasser Arafat of the Palestine Liberation Organization shake hands after the signing of a peace accord on September 13, 1993. Tragically, Rabin was assassinated while speaking at a peace rally in 1995, ending a long career of distinguished military and political service to Israel. Clinton joined many Americans in mourning his passing.

The Torah, a sacred parchment scroll consisting of the first five books of the Hebrew Bible, is central to the Jewish faith. Synagogues keep several of these scrolls, which are usually covered with rich fabric and silver ornamentation.

Passover, celebrated in the spring, is one of the most important Jewish holidays. Passover commemorates the Exodus, the enslaved Jews' flight from Egypt. Here, American Rabbi Marc Scheier leads a Passover service at the Chorale Synagogue in Moscow in 1988.

On the first two evenings of Passover, a family participates in a festival meal called a seder. Above, an American family reads from the Haggadah, a book containing the narrative of the Exodus and the ritual of the seder, before eating the traditional meal consisting of unleavened bread (matzoth), bitter herbs (maror), and wine.

These children are celebrating the Jewish rites of passage, known as Bar Mitzvah (for the boy) and Bat Mitzvah (for the girl), which are held at age thirteen. During the service, the young man or woman reads a passage from the Torah in Hebrew in front of the synagogue congregation as evidence that he or she is an adult and ready to become a full member of the congregation.

Brighton Beach, a neighborhood in the borough of Brooklyn, New York, is home to a large population of Russian Jews who have immigrated to the United States. Above, a Brighton Beach resident at the Jewish Pride Festival views an exhibit recounting successful historical efforts to free Soviet Jews.

A World War II veteran of the Soviet Red Army, Lev Vinjica came to the United States seeking religious freedom. Vinjica now sells Russian handicrafts from his vendor's booth in Brighton Beach.

In Judaism, the synagogue, which literally means "assembly," is a gathering place for worship, prayer, and education. During the Shabbat, or Sabbath services, congregants read from a siddur, a book of Jewish prayers.

Designed by the world-renowned architect Frank Lloyd Wright, the Beth Shalom Synagogue in Elkins Park, Pennsylvania, symbolizes the rock of Mount Sinai, the mountain from which Moses descended with the Ten Commandments.

Founded by Baal-Shem-Tov in the 1700s, the Jewish religious movement of Hassidism emphasizes the mercy of God and the importance of joyous expression in worship. The most notable Hassidic community in the United States is composed of the Lubavitchers. Lubavitchers, like this father and daughter in Crown Heights, Brooklyn, are known for their outreach to other Jews.

Opened in April 1993, the Holocaust Museum in Washington, DC, commemorates the 6 million Jews and millions of others who lost their lives in the Holocaust of World War II. Among the three-floor museum's many exhibits are the Children's Wall, the Hall of Remembrance, and the Learning Center. Above, a visitor examines a display of photographs depicting Jewish Lithuanian victims of the Holocaust.

Paula Lebovics, a resident of Encino, California, sits next to a portrait of her family. Lebovics and her family were sent to the Auschwitz concentration camp in Poland when she was a young girl. She survived, but several of her relatives were killed. In the portrait, her family members can be seen wearing the gold stars of David required by the Nazi regime to mark them as Jews. Lebovics is front and center in the portrait.

Film director and producer Steven Spielberg won both popular and critical acclaim for his 1993 film *Schindler's List*, based on the true story of a wealthy German industrialist who helped save the lives of more than 1,000 Jews during World War II. Spielberg has directed some of the highest-grossing motion pictures of all time, including *Jaws, E.T.,* and *Jurassic Park.*

Ruth Bader Ginsburg's distinguished career in law has been characterized by her contributions to the struggle for legal rights for women. On August 3, 1993, the Senate confirmed President Clinton's nomination of Ginsburg, making her the second woman in history to serve on the U.S. Supreme Court.

Share Information

Genealogists are a worldwide team, united by their interest and by the fact that they need each other's help. You may not be able to travel to Eastern Europe to trace your family's records in a certain town. But another amateur genealogist may live right there. You can get his or her name through several organizations or genealogical publications. Write or fax a letter, or put out a request on computer e-mail. You're likely to get the job done. But you must be willing to repay the favor when others ask you to check on something in your area.

You may also make a find of more general interest; a set of records, for example, that no one knew existed but that can benefit many.

Notify the groups you've worked with, or post the information on a computer genealogy bulletin board. See the **Resources** for this chapter. Others will do the same for you.

Be sure to share what you've learned with the members of your family and others who've helped you in the search. Not only do you owe it to them, but you will be repaid with even more cooperation the next time you ask for it.

Document Everything

If you've ever had trouble reading a road map, you know how frustrating it can be. The road network leading into the past can be much more complicated. There are numberless paths to follow, countless stories to check on, and an endless parade of characters passing through your family's drama.

The only way to keep track of where you've been, whom you've talked to, and what was said is to keep careful records. There are several formats for doing so. Some are discussed in this book. Whether you use these specially designed systems or just keep a careful diary of each step and its results, you must keep records.

Records should be kept of the dates of each action you take and each contact you make; the name and complete address, including phone, fax, or e-mail numbers of each contact and of the person or source who referred you to the contact; and dates and numbers of any documents.

You should keep copies of documents found, as well as copies of all tape recordings made and photos taken. Make a list of these items, giving the date, place, circumstances under which you found or created them, and a brief summary of what the item shows or tells, and why it's important.

You should keep a record of each piece of evidence with the material it supports. Note who gave you the confirmation or where it was found.

The best time to make these records is right after each step in the process, while your memory is fresh.

Of course, that raises the question of where to store all this information, which can reach quite a volume in a short time.

The simplest answer is an ordinary three-ring binder used only for your family history project. The rings allow you to add or remove material as you progress. We'll suggest a way to set this up below.

Getting Started

The first step in researching your family's background is to simply stop and think. You have some basic decisions to make that will greatly influence how much you do and how successful you are.

Do you want to know your background on your father's side? Your mother's? Or both? Are uncles, aunts, or cousins important to your project? These will be sidesteps on your family tree and will increase the size of your study and the effort it takes. What about second cousins and those beyond?

Will you be satisfied in knowing your family history from the time it began in the United States, or do you wish to pursue your research to Europe or other parts of the world? This would be rewarding, but would add to the study's difficulty.

Get a realistic idea of what you're trying to do before you try to do it. You can enlarge or reduce your goals later, depending on developments, but it's wise to have a finishing point in mind when you start. More genealogical projects fail because they are not realistic than for almost any other reason.

What Do You Know?

Begin by writing down everything you know—your name, your parents' names, and those of your uncles, aunts, cousins, and grandparents. Now list their addresses, phone numbers, and dates of birth, marriage, and death (if they are no longer living).

One means of organizing these data is by generations. Let the dividers in your ring binder separate your generation from that of your parents, their generation from that of your grandparents, and so on.

In each section, start a separate note sheet for each person or branch of the family. Or better yet, insert a letter-sized manila envelope (the kind that closes with a metal tab) for each. Punch three holes into one side of the envelope so it fits the rings in the binder.

Into this envelope place everything you know or can find out about the subject, on as many sheets of paper as needed. (Add additional envelopes as needed.)

You will probably also want to make use of two standard formats known and loved by genealogists—the family group sheet and the pedigree chart.

The family group sheet records information on one family —parents and children—with their names, birth dates, and places.

The pedigree chart weaves these separate elements into a kind of reverse family tree that starts with you and branches backward, first to your parents, then their parents, then their parents, and so on. This differs from a true family tree, which starts with one individual, then shows forward branching to his or her children, then their children, and so on. Pedigrees are usually laid out horizontally. Family trees stand upright, as a proper tree should. Further along in this book, you'll find a detailed description of how to fill out these charts. Right at the outset, though, these charts should be inserted in the front of your binder and filled out as much as possible with known information.

One of the goals in your genealogical search may be to pinpoint the country and city from which your ancestors emigrated—something that may be quite challenging, considering the vastness of the Jewish Diaspora. These Jewish children wave excitedly as the Statue of Liberty comes into view behind them. They were among fifty children from Vienna, Austria, who arrived in the United States in 1939 to be adopted by American families.

As you begin to build them, you'll find these charts can cover a lot of generations. Using Bible stories and commentaries, one enterprising Jewish genealogist actually stretched his "pedigree" all the way back to Adam and Eve. But it's fairly doubtful that he had two sources to confirm the majority of his steps, and likely no proof at all for others.

How far back into your family's history should your pedigree go? There is no fixed answer. Go back as far as you'd like to go or can go, depending on the time and other resources you can spend on the project; on what level of proof you're comfortable with; and on what you're trying to learn.

For a young Jewish American who now knows only that his or her grandparents came from "Poland or maybe Russia," finding the specific country is a goal. Finding the specific town in that country would be a triumph.

It might be possible to trace further if you were willing to travel to Europe, locate the records, and then find a translator for those records. It might be worth doing if, for example, a major claim to family wealth or historical importance were involved. For most people, that won't be the case. If you can trace your family back to your grandparents or great-grandparents, find out about their lives, and perhaps get in touch with family members you don't know or barely know, you'll have accomplished a great deal.

In any genealogical study, consider others involved in your life. Not all loved ones will share your passion for the past—some, in fact, may prefer not to discuss it. Though most will cooperate in answering your questions, that won't always be the case. Consider the needs and wants of those who care about you.

Phone Books

There is an electronic database that can help you find little-known family members, though it's pretty low-tech: the common telephone book. If your family name is unusual, it's sometimes worthwhile to check phone books for like-named people, especially in areas with large Jewish communities such as New York, Chicago, Los Angeles, Dallas, and Atlanta.

But why limit your search? These days, you can search virtually every U.S. phone book without ever leaving your computer screen. Using the information-carrying power of CD-ROMs, publishers have loaded almost all the books on disc—more than 70 million names. These programs can be purchased from the companies listed in the **Resources** section. You may want to talk to your local librarian about ordering a set of discs. Some online services such as CompuServe also offer access to the information.

Note, however, that locating people through phone books is far from a perfect process. The names and addresses may be misspelled or the persons may have moved by the time you find them.

There is also no guarantee that a person with your last

name is related to you, especially if you have a common Jewish name like Cohen, Levy, or Silverman.

What's the next step? Try calling them. Tell them your name, and you'll immediately have something in common. Then tell them what you are trying to do. If the call lasts more than ten minutes, you'll probably have a lot to talk about.

Filling Out Pedigree Charts and Family Group Sheets

As we said earlier, you're free to set up the recordkeeping of your family history project in any way that works for you. However, there are two forms that are standard in the genealogical world and that most organizations would ask to see before recognizing the work you've done. These are the pedigree and family history sheets mentioned earlier. Blanks are available at some stationery stores, and some books on genealogy have granted permission to copy their charts. Be careful not to copy any materials in which such permission has not been given. You may make copies of the forms provided in this book.

The Pedigree Chart

This chart is similar to the family tree but actually works in the opposite direction. A family tree starts with some individual in your past, then shows his or her children, their children, and so on. It's usually laid out vertically, like a tree. A pedigree, which is laid out horizontally, starts with you, then charts your parents, their parents, and so on.

The pedigree version shown here is the direct ancestor chart. Your name goes in the number 1 position. Numbers 2 and 3 are your father and mother, respectively (starting with 2, even numbers are male, odd numbers are female). Your father's parents are 4 and 5, your mother's parents 6 and 7, and so on back from there.

As you can see, even this simple direct-line chart can get pretty complex. Your two parents lead to four grandparents,

Pedigree Chart

Name of Compiler _____

Address _____

City, State _____

Date _____

Person No.1 on this chart is the same person as No.____ on chart No.____.

Chart No.____

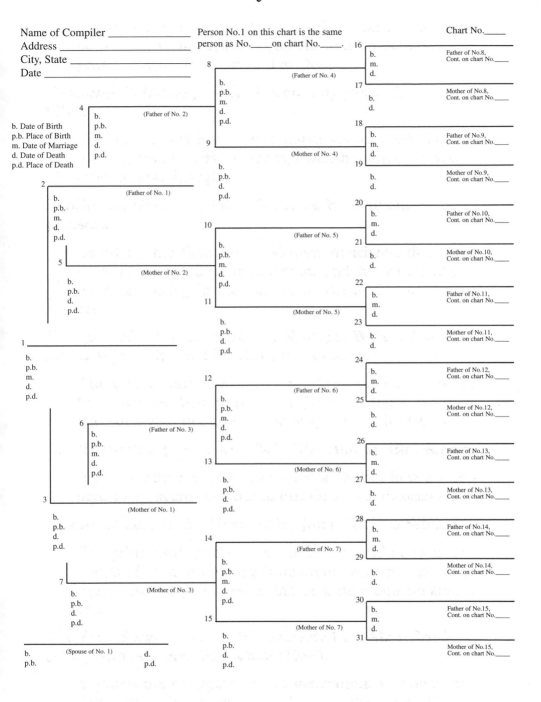

b. Date of Birth
p.b. Place of Birth
m. Date of Marriage
d. Date of Death
p.d. Place of Death

8

(Father of No. 4)
b.
p.b.
m.
d.
p.d.

4   (Father of No. 2)
b.
p.b.
m.
d.
p.d.

9

(Mother of No. 4)
b.
p.b.
d.
p.d.

2   (Father of No. 1)
b.
p.b.
m.
d.
p.d.

10

(Father of No. 5)
b.
p.b.
m.
d.
p.d.

5

(Mother of No. 2)
b.
p.b.
d.
p.d.

11

(Mother of No. 5)
b.
p.b.
d.
p.d.

1 _____
b.
p.b.
m.
d.
p.d.

12

(Father of No. 6)
b.
p.b.
m.
d.
p.d.

6   (Father of No. 3)
b.
p.b.
m.
d.
p.d.

13

(Mother of No. 6)
b.
p.b.
d.
p.d.

3
b.
p.b.
d.
p.d.

(Mother of No. 1)

14

(Father of No. 7)
b.
p.b.
m.
d.
p.d.

7   (Mother of No. 3)
b.
p.b.
d.
p.d.

15

(Mother of No. 7)
b.
p.b.
d.
p.d.

(Spouse of No. 1)
b.
p.b.
d.
p.d.

16
b.
m.
d.
Father of No.8,
Cont. on chart No.____

17
b.
d.
Mother of No.8,
Cont. on chart No.____

18
b.
m.
d.
Father of No.9,
Cont. on chart No.____

19
b.
d.
Mother of No.9,
Cont. on chart No.____

20
b.
m.
d.
Father of No.10,
Cont. on chart No.____

21
b.
d.
Mother of No.10,
Cont. on chart No.____

22
b.
m.
d.
Father of No.11,
Cont. on chart No.____

23
b.
d.
Mother of No.11,
Cont. on chart No.____

24
b.
m.
d.
Father of No.12,
Cont. on chart No.____

25
b.
d.
Mother of No.12,
Cont. on chart No.____

26
b.
m.
d.
Father of No.13,
Cont. on chart No.____

27
b.
d.
Mother of No.13,
Cont. on chart No.____

28
b.
m.
d.
Father of No.14,
Cont. on chart No.____

29
b.
d.
Mother of No.14,
Cont. on chart No.____

30
b.
m.
d.
Father of No.15,
Cont. on chart No.____

31
b.
d.
Mother of No.15,
Cont. on chart No.____

and eight great-grandparents. The next levels would have sixteen names, then thirty-two, then sixty-four, and so on. But most of these charts are limited to four generations. Most people of immigrant ancestry can't trace back much further.

Though all you need on the chart are names and numbers, genealogists also list important information in small print under the name so that the key data is in one place. This key information includes dates of birth and death, and dates of marriage and divorce if there were multiple marriages, as well as the names of spouses and children. The names of former spouses not on the chart are also in the small notes, as they were once in the family.

Genealogists use a simple code for this information:

b.	born
d.	died
d.unm.	died unmarried
d.s.p.	died without children
dau.	daughter
s.	son
div.	divorced
unm.	unmarried
=	married
I	left descendants

One important point in making these charts is always to keep the same number with the same person, no matter how many charts you make. Thus a person on a new chart can be linked to the same person on previous charts.

You can cross-reference the charts. Your maternal grandfather who is part of your history at number 6 on Chart A might have his own history on Chart B. Chart B would start at number 6. Each chart would carry a note referring to other charts on which he appears.

For a sample entry, let's go back to your maternal grandfather. If his name was Max Blum, and he married Sarah Sokol, and their only child was your mother, Leah, the note might look like this.

#6 MAX BLUM
   b. 10/5/25, Odessa, Russia
   d. 6/30/95, Los Angeles, CA
   = Sarah Sokol, 5/28/55, New York, NY
   dau. Leah, b. 5/8/58, Los Angeles, CA

Family Group Charts

If you wondered where to put all those sisters, brothers, aunts, uncles, and cousins, put them on your family group charts, also known as family group work sheets. These are simple listings of each family unit—one mother, one father, and all their children. (See the sample on page 98.) Include on these charts birth, marriage, and death dates and places for each person, as well as names of spouses. You can also include such nuggets of information as time and place of military service, place of burial, occupation, hobbies, accomplishments, favorite foods, and anything else you want to remember about family members.

Now simply give the mother and father the same numbers on the family group charts that they have on the pedigree. Result: You can travel back over the branches of the pedigree, stop at any individual, and look up his or her family group work sheet. Instantly you've accessed information on the children and detail on the parents.

Libraries and Interlibrary Loan

Your local public library, or a larger regional library, should be one of your first stops on your genealogical search.

If your family has lived in one city or state for many generations, the local history section of your public library may be useful to you. You may be able to learn about your relatives' involvement in local organizations and events or spot them in old newspapers or photos.

Check your local library for books on Jewish history and culture, as well as more specific genealogical materials. Larger libraries often have genealogical departments. If you are unsure how to begin using the library, ask the librarians. It is their job to help you find the materials you need, and

FAMILY GROUP WORK SHEET #_____

HUSBAND, Name: WIFE, Name:
Birth: Place: Birth: Place:
Death: Place: Death: Place:
Burial: Place: Burial: Place:
Father: Father:
Mother: Mother:
Occupation: Occupation:
Notes: Notes:

Name	Date & Place of Birth	Date & Place of Marriage	Date & Place of Death	Married to	Date & Place of Birth Death

they will be eager to do so. If certain books or other sources are not available at your library, ask your librarian about interlibrary loan. This service allows patrons to borrow materials from other libraries through their own local library, often free of charge.

Resources

JEWISH AMERICAN GENEALOGY

Avotaynu: The International Review of Jewish Genealogy.

Published quarterly, this is the best publication on the topic. Includes new sources, research tips, book reviews, and an "Ask the Experts" column. Subscriptions are $29. Back issues are $8 each. If you're online, you can get an index of ten years of articles by sending a blank e-mail message to avindex@cgsg.com. Or write or call:

Avotaynu, Inc.
155 North Washington Avenue
Bergenfield, NJ 07621
201-387-7200 or 1-800-AVOTAYNU.

Guzik, Estelle, ed. *Genealogical Resources in the New York Metropolitan Area*. New York: Jewish Genealogical Society, 1989.

With the largest Jewish population in the United States, the New York area is also home to many resources, detailed in this guide.

Isaacs, Ronald H., and Isaacs, Leora W. *Reflections: A Jewish Grandparent's Gift of Memories*. Northvale, NJ: Jason Aronson, 1987.

Especially useful for the forms it includes to organize your efforts.

Jacobsen, Howard. *Roots, Schmoots: Journeys Among Jews*. Woodstock, NY: Overlook Press, 1994.

Humorous look at a British writer's travels in search of his eastern European family origins. The search takes him through Israel, New York City, and even the Catskill Mountains summer resorts that New York Jews favored.

Kurzweil, Arthur, ed. *The Encyclopedia of Jewish Genealogy, Volume I: Sources in the United States and Canada*. Northvale, NJ: Jason Aronson, 1991.

Guide to U.S. and Canadian information sources. Additional volumes are in development.

————. *From Generation to Generation: How to Trace Your Jewish Genealogy and Personal History*, rev. ed. New York: HarperCollins, 1994.

First published in 1980, this is the "must have" book on the subject. It includes a full review of key ideas and sources, including both publications and archives, plus the author's account of how he found his own eastern European roots.

————. *My Generations: A Course in Jewish Family History*. New York: Behrman House, 1983.

Compact "handbook" version of his other works, written for young people.

Rosenstein, Neil. *The Unbroken Chain*. New York: CIS Publishers, 1990.

Biographical sketches and genealogies of key Jewish families from the 1400s to the present. Bibliographical notes and indexes.

Rottenberg, Dan. *Finding Our Fathers: A Guidebook to Jewish Genealogy*. Baltimore: Genealogical Publishing Co., 1986.

Almost as good as the Kurzweil book, and covering much of the same ground. Rothenberg's work suffers from out-of-date material. Includes a long listing of Jewish surnames, their meanings and their histories.

Stern, Malcolm H. *First American Jewish Families.* **Baltimore: Ottenheimer Publications, 1991.**

Written by one of the founders of Jewish American genealogy, this is the key work for researching the first Jews in America. Includes profiles of more than 50,000 individuals who settled before 1840 and how their families have developed to the present.

Zubatsky, David S., and Berent, Irwin M. *Jewish Genealogy: A Source Book of Family Histories and Genealogies,* **2 vols. New York: Garland, 1984, 1991.**

Lists genealogies already published, arranged by last name. A third volume is being compiled.

GENERAL GENEALOGICAL REFERENCES

Allen, Desmond Walls, and Billingsley, Carolyn Earle. *Beginner's Guide to Family History Research.* **Bountiful, UT: American Genealogical Lending Library, 1991.**

The authors, professional genealogists, introduce beginners to the building blocks of genealogical research. They cover topics such as searching home and family sources; systems of organizing records; using libraries and archives; searching census, courthouse, and military records; and correspondence. A glossary defines many of the terms you may encounter during your research.

Baxter, Angus. *Tracing Your European Roots.* **Baltimore: Genealogical Publishing Co., 1994.**

All-in-one reference guide to European information sources.

Bentley, Elizabeth P. *Directory of Family Associations.* **Baltimore: Genealogical Publishing Co., 1993.**

Large families sometimes form groups to coordinate history and stage reunions, as well as to offer help to family members. Jewish associations may be called "family circles."

————. *Genealogist's Address Book*. Baltimore: Genealogical Publishing Co., 1995.

A genealogy "yellow pages," filled with contact information for organizations and resources in the field.

Dollarhide, William. *Managing a Genealogical Project*. **Baltimore: Genealogical Publishing Co., 1988.**

Provides a unique system of organization for your genealogy project from the beginning stages to the end. Also includes a set of master forms that can be copied as often as needed.

Eichholz, Alice, ed. *Ancestry's Red Book: American State, County and Town Sources*, **rev. ed. Salt Lake City: Ancestry, Inc., 1992.**

Basic book explaining how to find, approach, and obtain information from local town clerks and courthouse recordkeeping agencies.

Genealogical & Local History Books in Print, 5th Edition. **Baltimore: Genealogical Publishing Co., 1996.**

Usually referred to as "G&LHBIP," this is the most complete listing of genealogical publications available: books, periodicals, privately published family histories, pedigrees, and family newsletters. The work is published in multiple volumes.

Greenwood, Val D. *The Researcher's Guide to American Genealogy*, **2d ed. Baltimore: Genealogical Publishing Co., 1990.**

Covers the basic principles and methods of genealogy, though not the immigration sources most useful for searching Jewish family history.

Kemp, Thomas J. *International Vital Records Handbook*. **Baltimore: Genealogical Publishing Co., 1994.**

Offers sources in all fifty states and many foreign nations, and includes the application forms to get them.

Stevenson, Noel C. *Genealogical Evidence: A Guide to the Standard of Proof Relating to Pedigrees, Ancestry, Heirship and Family History*, **rev. ed. Laguna Hills, CA: Aegean Park Press, 1989.**

What kinds of evidence do you need to trace your family history? What is considered valid proof by genealogists? This guide will help you to evaluate whether or not evidence is useful to you.

Wolfman, Ira. *Do People Grow on Family Trees? Genealogy for Kids and Other Beginners.* **New York: Workman Publishing, 1991.**

Classified as a children's book, this basic text is worthwhile reading for any age. Gives the principles of study and key recordkeeping formats.

Wright, Norman E. *Preserving Your American Heritage.* **Provo, UT: Brigham Young University Press, 1981.**

Wright describes a variety of genealogical records and provides advice on how to use them.

JEWISH GENEALOGICAL SOCIETIES (JGSs)

Every hobby has "clubs," in which members share information and experiences and help each other. Jewish genealogy has societies, more than fifty worldwide, with branches in forty U.S. cities, and in Canada, Israel, and several European nations. Most of the societies hold beginner classes and publish newsletters. To find the JGS nearest you, send a stamped, self-addressed envelope to:

Association of Jewish Genealogical Societies (AJGS)
155 North Washington Avenue
Bergenfield, NJ 07621

If you are online, you can send an e-mail message to jgs@cgsg.com. The addresses of all JGS chapters are published annually in the spring issue of *Avotaynu*. Some of the larger chapters are:

JGS of Los Angeles
P.O. Box 55443
Sherman Oaks, CA 91343
818-784-7277

JGS of Illinois
P.O. Box 515
Northbrook, IL 60065
708-679-1995

JGS of Greater Boston
P.O. Box 610366
Newton Highlands, MA 02161-0003
617-784-0387

Jewish Genealogical Society, Inc.
P.O. Box 6398
New York, NY 10128
212-330-8257

JGS of Cleveland
996 Eastlawn Drive
Highland Heights, OH 44143
216-449-2326

JGS of Philadelphia
332 Harrison Avenue
Elkins Park, PA 19117–2662
215-635-3263

JGS of Greater Washington
P.O. Box 412
Vienna, VA 22183–0412
301-654-5524

JGS of Canada
P.O. Box 446, Station A
Willowdale, Ontario M2N 5T1

Canada
416-638-3280

JGS **of Great Britain**
36 Woodstock Road, Golders Green
London NW 11 8ER
United Kingdom
081-455-3323

AMERICAN GENEALOGICAL SOCIETIES

American Genealogical Lending Library (AGLL)
593 West North Street
P.O. Box 329
Bountiful, UT 84011

Members of this organization can rent or buy microforms and CD-ROMs of vital records and census indexes for a reasonable fee. Check to see if your library is a member, or write AGLL about costs and terms of membership.

Meyer, Mary K. *Meyer's Directory of Genealogical Societies in the USA and Canada*, **7th ed. Mt. Airy, MD: M.K. Meyer, 1988.**

Genealogical societies can be useful sources of information as well as provide opportunities to "network" with other genealogists. This directory can lead you to genealogical societies in your area, or societies that focus on a topic you are interested in.

National Genealogical Society (NGS)
4527 17th Street North
Arlington, VA 22207-2363

A variety of forms, research aids, and books can be purchased from NGS. Membership includes a subscription to the *National Genealogical Society Quarterly* and the NGS *Newsletter*. They also offer a home study course, *American Genealogy: A Basic Course*. Write for information.

National Institute on Genealogical Research
P.O. Box 14274
Washington, DC 20044-4274

While members of this organization tend to be experienced genealogists, the institute offers many publications and workshops that you may find useful.

SPECIAL INTEREST GROUPS (SIGs)

For help in researching ancestors in a specific country or region, there are Special Interest Groups, or SIGs. Most have their own publications. Following are some of the largest groups, with the publications they offer:

Galicia (southern Poland and western Ukraine):

The Galitzianer, $15/year
c/o Suzan Wynne
3128 Brooklawn Terrace
Chevy Chase, MD 20815

Germany:

Stammbaum, $20/year
c/o Harry Katzman
1601 Cougar Court
Winter Springs, FL 32708-3855
e-mail: landsmen@cgsg.com

Hungary:

Magyar Zsido, $10/year
H-SIG
c/o Louis Schonfeld
P.O. Box 34152
Cleveland, OH 44134-0852
216-661-3970
e-mail: LouSMagyar@aol.com

Romania:

ROM-Sig News, $20/year
c/o Gene Starn
P.O. Box 520583
Longwood, FL 32752
407-788-3898

Southwest Lithuania and northeast Poland:

Landsmen, $22/year
c/o Marlene Silverman
3701 Connecticut Avenue NW, Apt. 228
Washington, DC 20008
e-mail: landsmen@cgse.com

JEWISH GENEALOGICAL FAMILY FINDER (JGFF)

Using the JGFF, you can find out if other researchers are looking for the same information as you are and contact them to work together. The program is updated several times yearly. The manager is Gary Motomoff of the New York JGS. All Jewish Genealogical Societies can produce a printout of the JGFF that you can examine. It can be purchased from Avotaynu, Inc. for $40. Write them at:

Jewish Genealogical Family Finder
155 North Washington Avenue
Bergenfield, NJ 07621

JEWISH GENEALOGICAL PEOPLE FINDER (JGPF)

The JGPF contains birth dates and places, death dates and places, parents' names and spouse's names for individual people. The information comes from family trees submitted by genealogists. More than 300,000 individuals are included. The JGPF can also be obtained from Avotaynu, Inc. or examined at Jewish Genealogical Societies.

ARCHIVES

American Jewish Archives
3101 Clifton Avenue
Cincinnati, OH 45220
513-221-1875

American Jewish Historical Society
2 Thornton Road
Waltham, MA 02154
617-891-8110

Central Archives for the History of the Jewish People
P.O. Box 1149
91010 Jerusalem, Israel

Leo Baeck Institute (German Jewry)
129 East 73rd Street
New York, NY 10021
212-744-6400

YIVO Institute (East European Jewry)
555 West 57th Street
New York, NY 10019

FAMILY HISTORY SOFTWARE

Brother's Keeper, version 5.2
John Steed
6907 Chilsdale Road
Rockford, MI 49341
616-364-5503

> Said to be difficult for beginners. There is a $45 shareware fee.

Family Tree Maker
Banner Blue Software
P.O. Box 7865
Fremont, CA 94537-7865
510-794-6850
e-mail: bbs1@aol.com.

Easy to use and ideal for beginners. DOS (4.0) and Windows (2.0) versions are $39.

The Master Genealogist
TMG 1.2.
Wholly Genes Software, Inc.
6868 Ducketts Lane
Elk Ridge, MD
800-982-2103
e-mail: 76366.1760@CompuServe.com.

Personal Ancestral File (PAF), version 2.31
Salt Lake Distribution Center
1999 West 1700 South
Salt Lake City, UT 84104
801-240-2584

Personal Ancestral File is the official software of the Mormon Church. It is not ideal for the way Jewish families are arranged. The DOS and Mac versions are $35.

Reunion (for Mac); and Reunion for Windows
Mac Connection: 800-800-1111
PC Connection: 800-800-5555

The Mac and Windows versions are $99.

Leister Productions
P.O. Box 289
Mechanicsburg, PA 17055
717-697-1378
e-mail: LeisterPro@aol.com.

Some call this the best program for use with Macintosh computers. It's especially good at making charts.

Roots IV
Commsoft
P.O. Box 310
Windsor, CA 95492
800-327-6687

This software costs $195.

GUIDES TO CHOOSING AND USING SOFTWARE

Archer, George W. *Archer's Directory of Genealogical Software.* **Bowie, MD: Heritage Press, 1994.**

———. *Archer's Directory of Genealogical Utility Software.* **Bowie, MD: Heritage Press, 1994.**

These directories will help you find information on many different programs.

Clifford, Karen. *Genealogy and Computers for the Complete Beginner: A Step-by-Step Guide to the* PAF *Computer Program, Automated Data Bases, Family History Centers, and Local Sources.* **Baltimore, MD: Clearfield Company, 1995.**

Introduces you to the vast resources of the Church of Jesus Christ of Latter-day Saints through the Personal Ancestry File. Also explains how to obtain records from the LDS Family History Centers.

Genealogical Computing (quarterly)
Ancestry, Inc.
P.O. Box 476
Salt Lake City, UT 84110
800-531-1790

Pence, Richard A., ed. *Computer Genealogy: A Guide to Research through High Technology*, **rev. ed. Salt Lake City: Ancestry, Inc., 1991.**

A discussion of the role of computers in genealogical research.

Przecha, Donna, and Lowrey, Joan. *Guide to Genealogy Software.* **Baltimore: Genealogical Publishing Co., 1993.**

The authors list and evaluate a broad variety of software options.

INTERNET RESOURCES

JEWISHGEN. Online discussion group on the subject of Jewish genealogy. Users can get help, post information, and communicate with other Jewish genealogists around the world. Contact JEWISHGEN through the newsgroup address: soc.genealogy.jewish.

To be put on an e-mail mailing list, send a message to listserv@mail.eworld.com. To submit a message other than a request to be connected, address: jewgen@mail.eworld.com. All subscribers will receive your message. There are now more than 700 members. There is no charge for the service, but members are asked to donate $25 a year.

Jewish Genealogy Home Page
http://dc.smu.edu/dvjcc/dvjcc.genealogy.html

Sponsored by the Dallas Jewish Historical Society, this home page is an excellent tool for researching Jewish genealogy in cyberspace. Includes links to general genealogy sites as well as those focusing specifically on Jewish genealogy.

Everton Publishers Genealogy Page
http://www.everton.com

This page contains information on getting started as well as specific information on ethnic, religious, and social groups. Includes an online edition of the genealogical magazine *Everton's Genealogical Helper* and provides links to archives, libraries, and other Internet resources.

Genealogy Home Page
http://ftp.cac.psu.edu/~saw/genealogy.html

By filling out the survey linked to this home page, you will be granted access to many genealogical links, allowing you to communicate with other genealogists, search new databases, and order genealogical software online.

LDS Research Guides
ftp://hipp.etsu.edu/pub/genealogy

This site focuses on the Research Outline Guides produced by the Family History Library in Salt Lake City. Subjects include getting started, frequently asked genealogy questions, and techniques for photograph dating.

National Archives and Records Administration (NARA)
gopher://gopher.nara.gov
http://www.nara.gov

NARA is the government agency responsible for managing the records of the federal government. Through this page you can find the location and business hours for regional archives or access information on finding and using particular government documents.

U.S. Census Bureau
http://www.census.gov

From this site you can access statistics about population, housing, economy, and geography as compiled by the U.S. Department of Commerce Bureau of the Census. You can also do specific word searches according to subject or geographic location.

World Wide Web Genealogy Demo Page
http://demo.genweb.org/gene/genedemo.html

This page is still under construction, but its goal is to "create a coordinated, interlinked, distributed worldwide genealogy database." Even in its incomplete form, Gen Web allows you to access all known genealogical databases searchable through the www.

Internet "sites" appear and disappear almost on a day-to-day basis without warning. If the above listings don't work, use the "search" key on your software to check for the organization's name. If not found, the material may no longer be offered or the organization may no longer exist. Check for new sites of interest by using the search terms "genealogy" and "Jewish genealogy."

PHONE BOOK CD-ROMS

PhoneDisc USA (2-disk set) is available for $49.50 from:

DAK Industries, Inc.
8200 Remmet Avenue
Canoga Park, CA 91304
800-325-0800

ProPhone (7-disk set) available for $129 from:

Better Business Systems
7949 Woodley Avenue
Van Nuys, CA 91406
818-376-1558

Chapter 8
Gaining Knowledge from Family Members

If you can't find what you want in life in your own backyard, the old saying goes, it probably doesn't exist. Genealogy can be like that. The greatest prizes of your family history usually lie, not in dusty libraries or government files, but in the hearts and memories of the members of your family. For that reason, genealogists agree that you should start the search for your family's past by first interviewing your own relatives.

How to Interview

An interview is vastly different from a conversation. It takes preparation, and you must know what you are looking for. What you get from the encounter will be no more than what you put into it.

Your goals should consist of the following four: Place each relative in the family pedigree—knowing who came before and after each and how they were related. Place each relative geographically, and in time, through the course of their lives. If your family member came from another country, or his or her parents were immigrants, as will usually be the case, you want to know from where, when, by what means, and with whom they traveled. Get information about other family members, especially if they're not available for interviews. Get ideas about others you should interview, or about sources to consult, such as a shipping line, hospital, or synagogue.

Your final goal is simply to let your subject talk. Interviewers are usually eager to get certain information, so they ask only about that information and keep pressing the point. This cuts off the subject's ability to tell you what he or she knows most about, which might be more interesting and

Cherishing knowledge received from one's elders is a Jewish tradition. At a home for elderly Jews, Allen Neihaus asks 93-year-old Hyman Tripp the four questions during a 1959 Passover seder.

useful than what you wanted. There's nothing as unproductive as an interview in which the questioner monopolizes the session.

During the interview, you should take notes. But making a tape recording of the conversation in addition to taking notes is even better, so you can concentrate on the question-and-answer process during the interview. It's also almost certain that you'll hear information on a later listening that you missed during the interview. Listen to your tape at least twice. Three times is even better.

If you have access to the proper equipment, you should consider recording your interviews on videotape. Years later, you will be able to see—and show your children—what your relatives were like. You'll also be able to compare their appearance at the time of the interview with earlier and later photos. Any keepsakes they show you during the talk will be on view as well.

What questions should you ask? That can vary, depending on what you already know or need to find out. In some interviews you'll be looking for details to fill in the blanks, or confirmation of what you've learned elsewhere. But if your interview happens early in your search, your questions should be basic.

Here are some basic questions to ask, as recommended by Arthur Kurzweil. Kurzweil tailored these questions for Jewish families with European roots, but they can be customized to those with other geographic backgrounds.

This list is paraphrased; consult the complete list on pp. 49–54 of the 1994 revised edition of Kurzweil's book *From Generation to Generation*.

- What town(s) did your family come from in Europe? Where were these towns located?
- Who were the immigrants to the United States in our family?
- What are the specific reasons your family came to the United States?
- If you were an immigrant, describe the trip to the United States.
- In what port did your ship dock? What was the name of the ship and the date it arrived?
- What was life like in Europe? What are some of your early childhood memories?
- What contact did your family maintain with the "old country"? Did you receive letters from relatives who remained there? Were those letters saved? May I see them? (Note that you are *not* asking "May I have them?")
- What were your parents' names? Your mother's maiden name? Your brothers' and sisters' names and order of birth? Their occupations?

- What do you remember about your grandparents and great-grandparents?
- Whom were you named after? What do you know about him or her?
- Where did your family live in the United States? What memories are especially vivid from your childhood?
- What do you remember about your first job? The living conditions at home as a child?
- Was your family religious? Were they Orthodox or Hasidic?
- If Hasidic, did they follow any particular *rebbe* (rabbi)?
- Did your family belong to a synagogue in the United States? Is there a family cemetery plot? Who bought or organized it?
- What do you remember about your childhood during holidays? Your *Bar* or *Bas Mitzvah*?
- Is there a family Bible? May I see it?
- Do you remember the *shul* (synagogue) in Europe? What was it like?
- Do you have your *ketubah* (marriage document)?
- Is there a family photo album? Old photographs? May I see any family keepsakes such as candlesticks, ceremonial *kiddish* cups, or *tefillin* (prayer boxes strapped on the head and arm during religious services)?
- Do you have your old passports? Citizenship papers? Birth certificate? Old letters, recipes, diaries, Bibles, books?
- Is there a written genealogy already in the family? (You'd be amazed how often family histories have already been done. If so, your work can add to it.)

Kurzweil also offers these suggestions to enhance the interviews:

- Interview twice on different days. The first day's questions will often jog memories the person hasn't thought about for years. During the second interview, these memories may come pouring forth.
- Phrase your questions to be answered with stories and

anecdotes, not yes or no replies. Ask "why", "what", and "how" questions.

- Have those who don't want to be interviewed present when willing interviewees are questioned. "The 'silent' one," says Kurzweil, "will often add his or her two cents."

- Use old photos to start the discussion. Ask who is shown, where the photo was taken, and why. Ask what happened before and after the time the photo was taken.

- Tell the people interviewed that you'll report your discoveries to them—then keep your promise. Send them a written copy of the interview and ask them to let you know of any additions or corrections.

Writing for Information

Often it's not possible or convenient to interview in person. Your subjects may live in other nations or faraway states, or have no time to talk to you. The alternative is the written interview.

It would seem simple to lay out all the questions above on one or two pages of a questionnaire. It's been done that way. But there's a downside, say those who've done it.

Family history is a personal thing. Those questioned may be unwilling to have their lives examined by an impersonal letter presenting a set of generic questions. Instead, follow these hints:

- Write your questions in a warmly written letter that clearly identifies you as a member of the family and tells what you are trying to do and why you want to do it.

- Promise to share your findings. (Follow through on that promise.)

- Ask only a few questions per letter. Make them as personalized as possible. If you know that your great-aunt came from Berlin, Germany, for example, you might ask specific questions about life there.

- Include a self-addressed, stamped envelope for the person to write you back. It will greatly increase your chances of getting a reply.

The following is a sample letter requesting information from a relative:

Your address

Date

Name of Relative
Address

Dear (Name of Relative),

I am in the process of preparing a history of our family. I hope to trace the first member of the family who left our native home and immigrated to the United States—and to follow the line down to the present generation.

I wonder if you would be so kind as to write me a letter describing your memories, how you came to live where you do, what other members of your family are living and, for those who have passed on, their places of burial.

Any anecdotes or stories about members of our family would also be very welcome.

Let me assure you that this is a purely personal project, intended only for myself and any interested family members. Any information you give me will be used solely for the family history.

I shall be glad to keep you informed of the progress of my project and to send you a copy of the final result.

It would be a great pleasure to hear from you and to include your information in the overall picture of our family. If you have any photographs or keepsakes that I could borrow, I promise that I will treat them with the greatest care and return them to you safely.

Hoping to hear from you,

Sincerely yours,

Your signature

Heirlooms, Keepsakes, and Antiques

While physical objects can't talk, they can provide plenty of information to the genealogist if you know what to look for. Here are some common objects that you may come across in a genealogical search:

- Photographs. These are extremely valuable. Examine the clothing and hairstyles of the subjects for clues to the date the photo was taken. If your subject wears traditional clothing or national dress, these are additional clues to the origin of the photo.

  The type of photo can indicate when it was taken. Black-and-white glossy prints known as "snapshots" are recent. They were probably made no earlier than the 1930s. Older photos had a brownish tone, called "sepia." They were more rigidly posed, as cameras tended to be bulky and seldom taken out of the studio. Studio photos are often marked with the name and address of the studio on the back.

  If the photo is of a street scene, note the vehicles. Are they motor vehicles, wagons, or a mix of both? If they are cars, how rounded are the body styles? The more streamlined, the more recent. In interior shots, look at the appliances and lighting, as well as the type and style of furniture and carpeting. Heavy, dark furniture and an oriental rug are hallmarks of the 1920s or earlier. Is there a telephone in the picture? The style might provide hints to the date the photo was taken.

- Books and periodicals. Books are a gold mine of information. First, most carry a copyright date and city, giving you the place and time of publication. The language of the book is a tipoff to the nationality of the owner; the subject tells of his or her interests; and the quality of the book can hint at the owner's economic status.

  Many books were also personalized with the owner's name, or a gift message, perhaps specifying the giver's relationship to the owner ("From Aunt

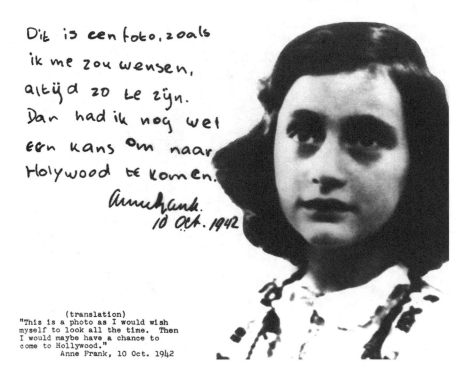

Dit is een foto, zoals
ik me zou wensen,
altijd zo te zijn.
Dan had ik nog wel
een kans om naar
Holywood te komen.
Annefrank.
10 Oct. 1942

(translation)
"This is a photo as I would wish
myself to look all the time. Then
I would maybe have a chance to
come to Hollywood."
Anne Frank, 10 Oct. 1942

Family keepsakes and memorabilia such as letters, diaries, photos, and religious articles can be valuable genealogical research materials. One of the most famous pieces of writing in Jewish history is the diary of Anne Frank, which documented her family's experiences hiding from the Nazis in Amsterdam. Above, a photo of Frank found in her diary.

Rachel," for example). Professional books, of course, can tell you about your forebears' occupations.

- Clothing and jewelry. Just as it does today, style can often tell you when clothing and jewelry were made and worn. Long, dark dresses, for example, gave way to short styles in the "flapper" era of the 1920s. Hats come in and out of style.

The cameo brooch was a standard of the early years of the twentieth century. And generally, the more the item of clothing covered the body, the older it is. Compare the items you've found to photos taken during the period you suspect they were made, and see if there's a match. In any item, look for labels that give you the place of manufacture or sale and for monograms, which can help identify the wearer. Mili-

Religious items such as ceremonial candlesticks, cups, and prayer shawls may have been handed down in your family for generations. Above, Mae Shafter Rockland of Brookline, Massachusetts, sets her family table for the Passover seder.

tary uniforms and decorations tell nationality, rank, and accomplishments, and can help you determine the years, places, and branches of the military in which your ancestors served. This can point you to their written records.

- Household and religious items. Jewish families tend to keep religious clothing items such as a *tallis* (prayer shawl), yarmulkes (skullcaps), and *tefillin* (small leather boxes containing Torah writings worn on the head and arm during morning prayer). They might also keep household items of religious importance such as *menorahs* or other ceremonial candlesticks, *mezuzahs* (a piece of the Torah encased in a container and placed on doorposts), and *kiddish* cups. These may be marked or embroidered with identifying marks or monograms.

Look also for such keepsakes as pocket watches or

bracelets, which may carry engraved messages, or items that indicate nationality such as the samovar, a tea-making machine with a spigot. Many Russian Jewish households brought this from Europe.

Musical instruments were also valued, and many families have kept a violin, accordion, or even a harmonica through many generations. These instruments may also carry a plate or plaque with the owner's name or initials. Certain instruments are native to a country or to one of its regions. The balalaika, for example, is a guitar-like stringed instrument from Russia.

- Tools of Trade. These can tell a great deal about your family's past. You may, for instance, find jeweler's tools, medical instruments, or building and farm implements. Their design, markings, materials, and quality are clues to when they were made and the professional status of the user.

- Toys. This is one of the most fascinating categories of past items. Dolls, especially, can be unique to historical periods, places, and even specific creators and are often prized by collectors.

If you are unable to identify an object's age or origin, try checking the catalogs of antique items at many libraries. You may not find the exact match, but you will probably be able to find something similar and get a general sense of when your item was made. Ask a librarian about antique books and catalogs.

Gravestones

Gravestones and other kinds of cemetery records can provide the genealogist with a wealth of information.

Jewish families often purchase family plots, so several members of a family, over several generations, will be buried together. Gravestone inscriptions often give the name of the father, and sometimes the name of the mother of the deceased. Year of birth and death are commonly engraved on the stone, as may be information such as "beloved husband of" or "dear wife of." Children are listed under "father of" or "mother of."

Most stones carry an epitaph, or final message about or by the deceased. Many of these are general ("He loved life"), but you may find a hint to the deceased's interests or occupation, or even political views. One stone, placed in honor of a Jewish teenager w--ho died in 1969 of an illness, carries a 1960s peace sign.

Plots are also purchased by organizations such as unions, family circles, fraternal organizations, and synagogues. Groups of people from the same town or region, called *Landsmannschaften,* also frequently purchase plots together. These organizations and their living members may have more information about the deceased.

How do you know where your relative was buried? Often that information is on the death certificate. You should also, of course, simply ask living relatives.

Information on gravestones may not always be accurate, however. The survivors may not actually know the facts when asked by the funeral director, or they may give wrong information under the stress of their loss. Sometimes the stonecutter makes an error. On older stones, the information may be weathered with age or even defaced.

Another difficulty is that the information on many Jewish stones is engraved in Hebrew. If you do not read Hebrew, ask a friend or relative who does to accompany you to the cemetery.

You can generally photograph gravestones when it does not interfere with cemetery activities, so there's no need to try to figure it all out at the gravesite. Check the cemetery's main office to find out if there are specific rules or guidelines you should follow. You may also make a rubbing, or tracing of the lettering, by coating the stone with a special wax, then laying paper over it and rubbing across the writing. An exact, full-sized image of the writing and design is transferred to the paper.

You can order grave-rubbing supplies and instructions from Oldstone Enterprises, 186 Lincoln Street, Boston, MA 02111.

Resources

INTERVIEWING AND ORAL HISTORY

Arthur, Stephen, and Arthur, Julia. *Your Life &*
Times: How to Put a Life Story on Tape. **Baltimore:**
Genealogical Publishing Co., 1987.

> Explains what kinds of things to include in an oral history
> and how to record it. Contains a list of questions that will
> lead you through the important events of your life.

Banaka, William H. *Training In Depth Interviewing.*
New York: Harper and Row, 1971.

> This book gives great interviewing tips, encompassing
> topics such as how to prepare for an interview, ways to
> keep the conversation focused, and how to get answers
> that will be helpful to you.

Bannister, Shala Mills. *Family Treasures: Videotaping*
Your Family History. **Baltimore: Clearfield Co., 1994.**

> Besides interview questions, the author provides sugges-
> tions for camera angles and equipment.

Gouldrup, Lawrence P. *Writing the Family Narrative.*
Salt Lake City: Ancestry, Inc., 1987.

> This how-to guide will help you organize your source
> material into a running narrative that is both informative
> and entertaining.

Harris, Ramon, et al. *The Practice of Oral History.*
Glen Rock, NJ: Microfilming Corporation of America,
1975.

> Includes many helpful appendixes, and full of advice,
> hints, and examples. Also suggests present and future uses
> of oral history.

Hoopes, James. *Oral History: An Introduction for Students*. Chapel Hill: University of North Carolina Press, 1979.

In-depth chapters on preparing, arranging, and holding interviews. Also contains an appendix of oral history collections and sources, and a bibliography.

Ives, Edward I. *The Tape-Recorded Interview: A Manual for Field Workers in Folklore and Oral History*. Knoxville: University of Tennessee Press, 1974.

A comprehensive manual for recording interviews on tape. Although the discussion of tape recorders is a bit outdated, the procedural issues the book covers are still relevant.

Kanin, Ruth. *Write the Story of Your Life*. Baltimore: Clearfield Co., 1993.

Finish your project off by interviewing yourself. After all, your story is the latest chapter of your family history. This book offers guidelines, samples, and pitfalls to avoid in telling your own story.

McLaughlin, Eve. *Interviewing Elderly Relatives*. Plymouth, UK: Federation of Family History Societies, 1985.

Contains good interviewing advice on conducting interviews with older subjects.

Muran, Lois Kay. *Family Tree Questionnaire*. Baltimore: Clearfield Co., 1995.

A series of fill-in-the-blank forms to ensure that your interview covers the most important bases.

GRAVESTONES

The Association for Gravestone Studies
46 Plymouth Road
Needham, MA 02192

Write for a brochure with information on books and leaflets about cemeteries and gravestones.

Schafer, Louis S. *Tombstones of Your Ancestors.* **Bowie, MD: Heritage Books, 1991.**

General guidance and detailed instructions on how to decipher gravestones and other cemetery records, and how to make copies to be examined at home.

Schumacher, Michael. *Creative Conversations: The Writer's Complete Guide to Conducting Interviews.* **Cincinnati: Writer's Digest Books, 1990.**

Young genealogical writers can learn much from this book, despite the fact that it is intended for professional writers. The first chapter, "The Interview and Its Uses," is especially helpful.

Stano, Michael E., and Reinsch, N. L., Jr. *Communication in Interviews.* **Englewood Cliffs, NJ: Prentice-Hall, 1982.**

Provides effective interviewing techniques, covering topics such as speaking clearly and assessing nonverbal signals from the interviewee.

Chapter 9
Searching for Records

In the simple act of living, the members of your family have left a paper trail at government offices across the United States and probably around the world. You can follow that trail to find out when and where they were born, married, and died, and also when and where they took such key steps as serving in the military or buying or selling land. All these key events are by law recorded with the government. The papers that hold this information are called vital records. Following are some of the key records and where to find them.

- Birth Certificates. The time and place of every birth is recorded by either a doctor or a religious authority. These records are kept at town or city departments of records. The certificate gives the parents' names, their address at the time, and other data. Give the clerk the name you're looking for and when you think the person was born, or if you know the approximate date, look it up in the large registry books kept by some agencies. The original certificate must stay in the file, but the clerk will make you a copy for a small fee.
- Death Certificates are issued for each death and are usually filled out by medical personnel or funeral directors. They give the deceased's name and address and the time, place, and cause of death, if known. They may also give the names of other family members and even the date and place of birth of the deceased and his or her parents' names. Death certificates are usually kept by the same agency that

handles birth certificates, or at the office of the coro-
ner, the town official in charge of determining cause
of death.

- Marriage Certificates. Completed by a rabbi if the
  ceremony was religious, or a town official or judge if
  not, these are also kept at the town records bureau.
  Marriage certificates give the date and place of marriage, and also the wife's maiden name. Don't confuse
  the official marriage certificate with the *ketubah*, the
  Hebrew document drawn up by a rabbi and given to
  the newlyweds. This often elaborate and sometimes
  illustrated certificate will probably be found in the
  married couple's personal records.
- Divorce Papers are not usually filed with the town
  records bureau. They are kept at the court that
  granted the divorce. These papers are often closed to
  inspection except by lawyers or the parties involved.

  If you can obtain them, divorce papers give a history of the marriage and the couple's backgrounds,
  names and ages of children, and lists of property, as
  well as the reason for the marital breakdown.

  Jews married by a rabbi are also supposed to obtain
  a Jewish divorce, called a *get*. This is a Hebrew document issued by a rabbi or court of rabbis. Like the
  ketubah, it is likely to be with the family records.

A booklet entitled "Where to Write for Vital Records" is
published by the U.S. Department of Health and Human
Services. It may be obtained from the U.S. Government
Printing Office, Washington, DC 20402-9325.

Social Security Death Index (SSDI)

Death records are also kept by the Social Security Adminis-
tration. The records are in a file called the Social Security
Death Index or SSDI.

This file contains the place and date of death of some 60
million Americans who died from 1962 on, had a social
security card, and whose families asked for benefits. The

SSDI is available on CD-ROM and can be examined free of charge through the Family History Centers of the Church of Jesus Christ of Latter-day Saints, which are explained later.

From the SSDI, you can learn your late relative's social security number. With the number, and a seven-dollar fee, you can order a copy of his or her original application for a social security card. The form you file is Form SS-5.

The application contains the person's date and place of birth, as well as both parents' full names. To order an SS-5, write to Freedom of Information Officer, 4H8 Annex Building, 6401 Security Boulevard, Baltimore, MD 21235.

Census Data and Military Records

Since 1790, the U.S. government has carried out a head-count of every American once every decade. This count is called the census. Its results are the official population figures for the United States.

During a census, tens of millions of questionnaires are mailed to households nationwide. Then officials, called census-takers, hit the streets to count those who can't be reached by mail. There is even an attempt made to count the homeless.

If your relatives lived in the United States during any census, chances are good that they were counted. The information collected includes names and ages for everyone living in a household and other data such as family health and income. One recent census even counted how many bathrooms each home had.

Census records are easy to use, but some are hard to obtain. To protect privacy, only records made through 1920 are open to public inspection. You must present a death certificate to see anything more recent.

Another difficulty is that many records up to and including 1890 were destroyed in a fire. But because so many Jewish families entered the United States between 1880 and 1925, it's very likely that members of your family entered the country then. Census records after 1890 may be a gold mine of information.

Census records are under the care of the National Archives, just a few blocks from the White House and Capitol
in Washington, DC.

This agency has many publications useful to genealogists.
They're described in a free booklet entitled "Aids for Genealogical Research." Write to Publications Distribution,
(NECD), Room G-9, National Archives, Washington, DC
20408.

The National Archives has thirteen Regional Archives.
Each has copies of the full censuses as well as other records.
The National Archives also has custody of military records
back to the Revolutionary War. If past family members
served in the U.S. armed forces, their records will likely be
on file. These will include dates and places of service, rank,
branch, and type of job.

Of even greater importance to Jewish Americans, the
Archives maintain lists of immigrants who won American
citizenship and passenger lists of ships that carried those
immigrants to the United States. These last two items are
described later.

Other records available at the National Archives include
land records, passport applications, personnel records for
civilian employees of the federal government, claims by
veterans and their widows or other dependents for pensions
or bounty land, and records for births, marriages, and deaths
that occurred at U.S. Army bases and U.S. Foreign Service
posts.

Many of the most heavily used records at the National
Archives have been microfilmed and are available at more
than one facility. Photocopies of most records can also be
obtained for a fee per page.

Family History Library

Another, perhaps surprising, major source for locating Jewish
vital records is the Church of Jesus Christ of Latter-day
Saints (LDS), or the Mormons.

The Mormons believe that a person may be enrolled in
their church even after death if a living relative of the de-

ceased is a member. For this reason, the Church has been extremely active in tracking family history.

They maintain the largest genealogical library in the world at LDS headquarters in Salt Lake City, Utah. Called the Family History Library (FHL), it contains nearly 2 million rolls of microfilm and a quarter of a million books.

The Library is open to persons of all faiths. Nine of every ten users are not Mormon.

The FHL has branches, called Family History Centers, at more than 2,000 local churches. Local centers can order materials from headquarters for a small fee. Check your telephone directory or call or write the FHL to find out if there is a Family History Center near you.

The FHL has copies of nearly everything that the National Archives does, as well as other items, such as local records, found in its "Locality" files. The Mormons have also converted to microfilm vital records of several Eastern European nations, including Poland, Germany, and Hungary. These include several thousand Jewish records. Russian Jewish records have yet to be collected.

The key to using the FHL is the Family History Library Catalog, or FHLC, which can be examined at Family History Centers. You can view instructional videos on "How to Use the FHLC" and "How to Use a Family History Center." These can be ordered for five dollars each from Salt Lake Distribution Center, 1999 West 1700 South, Salt Lake City, UT 84104. A "Family History Publications List" (#34083) of other research aids and services can also be ordered.

Shipping and Citizenship Papers

The paper trail of vital records your family members left will at some point stop at the water's edge. To continue to determine how your forebears got here and to trace their lives to a previous homeland, you need to uncover the documents of their voyage. These are shipping papers and immigration documents, both at the National Archives.

First, look into steamship passenger lists. Each ship that arrived was required to keep them and file them with government officials as a record of the voyage. If your relatives came by ship, their names and other valuable data will be on these records.

Passenger lists are categorized by port. If you're not sure which port to look for, try New York first. It was the gateway for some 24 million immigrants. Boston, Baltimore, Philadelphia, and New Orleans each processed fewer than 2 million newcomers.

National Archives records run from 1820 through the 1950s, depending on city, and indexes are available. If you know the date of arrival and the name of the ship, you can order a copy of the passenger list by using Form NATF-81. The search is free. A copy of the record costs ten dollars.

The Archives will do the search only if there is an index. The earliest years are not indexed. If you need to search one of those years, you'll have to look at every ship's record. Some private indexes are published. And the LDS Family History Center is indexing every New York passenger list from 1897 through 1924 on computer.

The Morton Allan Directory of European Passenger Steamship Arrivals lists every ship arrival at the major east coast ports during the years of most active immigration. Specific years depend on the port, but the range is from 1890 to 1930. If a relative can tell you the name of the ship he or she came on, this book will tell you where and when it landed.

Canadian Arrivals

Of course, not all immigrants entered the United States through a U.S. port. Some landed in a Canadian port, then made their way across the border.

Canada has records of ship arrivals, and the United States has records of persons passing over the border. The Canadian records are available from National Archives of Canada, 395 Wellington Street, Ottawa K1A 0N3, Canada.

Six ports, including Quebec and Halifax, are covered from the mid-1800s up to 1919. The lists are arranged by year. Records after 1920 are closed for privacy reasons. Questions may be addressed to Query Response Centre, Employment and Immigration Canada, 10th Floor, Place du Portage, Phase IV, Hull, Quebec K1A 0J9, Canada.

The U.S. Government lists of persons crossing from Canada are called St. Albans Lists. They cover 1895 to 1954 and are indexed. The lists and indexes are at the National Archives in Washington, at several Regional Archives, and at the LDS Family History Centers.

"First Papers . . . Final Papers"

You can often find the exact date and port of entry of your relative's arrival on his or her naturalization papers. These are the forms filed to gain U.S. citizenship. Look for these in your family records.

There are several documents. What most immigrants call "first papers" is a form entitled "Declaration of Intention." This was filed shortly after an immigrant landed. The form notified the government of a person's intention to become a citizen. An application for "final papers," called the "Petition for Naturalization," was filed five years later.

Every would-be citizen had to pass a test. They were asked "Who is the President?" and "How many U.S. states are there?" in addition to questions about how the government functioned. Those who passed were sworn in by a judge and handed a Certificate of Citizenship. Whatever they were when they walked in, they walked out as Americans.

New citizens often took the oath of citizenship in large groups, but everyone experienced it personally. Many former immigrants still point to the swearing-in as one of the high points of their lives.

Until 1922, spouses and children automatically became citizens when the head of the household did. Citizenship was also automatically obtained by marrying a citizen. If your relative tells you, "I became a citizen on my father's (or mother or spouse's) papers," that's what he or she means. After 1922, spouses had to file their own papers.

Naturalization papers give the name of applicant, date of entry, and date and place of birth—extremely valuable if you seek to find your European origins. The final application for

Many Jewish immigrants entered the United States through Ellis Island. In 1949, Jews who had been temporarily detained at Ellis Island still managed to celebrate the Succoth holiday, including the building of the Succah, a bough-covered hut.

citizenship gives the most information. If you can't find it among your family's records, the government maintains copies of all citizenship papers; however, it can take a year or more after a request is filed with the Immigration and Naturalization Service, the agency that stores the records, before receiving the requested papers. Genealogical experts suggest that you try contacting the court that handled the swearing-in ceremonies.

Ellis Island

From 1850 on, New York immigrants entered through Castle Garden, in downtown Manhattan, which was built as a fort and also once served as a concert hall. They received a medical exam and were questioned. Unless they were found to be ill or had some other problem, they were then released onto the streets of New York to start their new lives.

As the immigration wave crested, Castle Garden quickly became overcrowded. In 1892, the U.S. Government moved the entry station to a small island in New York harbor right next to the Statue of Liberty. Immigrants stepped off their steamships onto a ferryboat that took them to Ellis Island.

A writer at the time compared what happened on Ellis Island to a kind of Judgment Day. People stood in long lines before inspectors and received a quick medical inspection. If an inspector chalk-marked a newcomer's coat with a large H for heart trouble, or worse, an X for mental defects, it could mean going right back on the ship to Europe. Officials especially looked for tuberculosis, which they called the "Jewish disease."

As many as 15,000 immigrants passed through Ellis Island on a single day, though one-third that number was more typical. Before it shut down in 1954, 12 million new Americans entered through its gates.

These days most immigrants arrive by air. They're given appointments to appear at government office buildings for processing later.

Ellis Island is now a Museum of Immigration. Parts have been restored to their original state. It is well worth visiting. Or better yet, take your grandparents to visit it. One Jewish woman from Russia had been through Ellis Island at age twelve. Now sixty-five, she was treated to a visit by her children and grandchildren. She looked around the great waiting room where thousands had stood, luggage in hand and future on the line. Then she headed for a government-issue bench and sat down. "I sat right here till they called me for examination," she said in Yiddish-accented English. "*Right here!*"

Jewish Names

As you look through family history documents, keep in mind the record-keeping problems that arose from the names of European Jews. Officials of the time sometimes recorded

names with wrong spellings. Other names were simply short-
ened or replaced with an "American" name that sounded
somewhat the same. Schmit could become Smith; Ertzl
might be changed to Edwards.

Names were also lied about. Someone in the United
States, not a family member, would agree to accept an immigrant as a "son" or "nephew." The purpose might be to
use that person as a low-paid worker. The newcomer would
adopt his or her sponsor's name. Thus any attempt to
track the immigrant's family history ends up on a wrong
track.

An additional difficulty comes from often-heard names
such as Cohen or Rosenberg. Even if persons with the same
last name came from the same town, you cannot say they
were related, any more than you can say two people named
Smith from Boston are. The name is simply too common.

First names were also changed as new immigrants named
Hershl or Isaac became more "American" by calling themselves "Harry" or "Irv." First letters were often the same,
but they didn't have to be.

Bibliographers suggest using passenger lists as a way to get
around the problem of changed names. The lists were made
before arrival and therefore should carry the original name.

Where Jewish Names Came From

Actually, until the early 1800s, many poorer Jews did not
even have last names. They were simply "Yudl the begger"
or "Moshe the peddler." Others were known only as the
child of their parents. The *ovitch* at the end of many Russian
names means "son of." Alexandrovitch is therefore "the son
of Alexander." It's not a problem until one thinks of how
many Alexanders there were—and how many had sons!

Names can help you understand the sequence of birth and
death in your family. Ashkenazic Jews commonly name a
child after a deceased relative to honor the person's memory.
You can use the child's name as a pointer. Look a generation or two back in your family tree and you can expect to
see the same name on an ancestor. Recent generations have

kept up the custom, but in a way that allows the child a more "modern" name than the ancestor had. It's done by using the same first letter. If the ancestor was Esther, the child may be Ellen or Elisa. Middle names have also been devoted to the past relative. Check both first and middle names to see the relationship to ancestors.

Last names may also help tell you about the occupation or personal characteristics of your ancestors. If you know a Fleisher and a Becker, their ancestors may have been a butcher and a baker. The Rabinovich family somewhere along the line included the son of a rabbi. And the Cantor family included a cantor.

Resources

LIBRARIES AND ARCHIVES

Family History Library
35 North West Temple Street
Salt Lake City, UT 84150

This is the largest genealogical library in the world. Although it is affiliated with the Church of Jesus Christ of Latter-day Saints, anyone can take advantage of its massive resources and cutting-edge research technology. Many of their records are stored on microfilm and, in many cases, can also be accessed on CD-ROM. Local branches of FHL are called Family History Centers. Contact the main library or consult a phone book to find the location of the Family History Center near you.

Guide to Genealogical Research in the National Archives. **Washington, DC: National Archives and Records Service, 1985.**

Details the various services offered by the Archives, how to access them, and what charges, if any, are involved in using them.

Kaminkow, Marion J. *Genealogies in the Library of Congress: A Bibliography.* **2 vols. Baltimore: Magna Carta, 1972.**

It is possible that someone in your family has already done some research on your family history. If they had their work published, it may be contained in the Library of Congress collection. Check this bibliography to see whether some of your work might have already been done for you.

National Archives and Records Administration
Washington, DC 20408

The National Archives store censuses, vital records, and many other important documents. Among the free publications offered by the National Archives are *Military Service Records in the National Archives; Using Records in the National Archives for Genealogical Research;* and *Beginning Your Genealogical Research in the National Archives.*

Parker, J. Carlyle. *Going to Salt Lake City to Do Family History Research.* **Turlock, CA: Marietta Publishing Co., 1989.**

If you live near Salt Lake City, or if a family vacation takes you nearby, it might be worth your time to pay a visit to the Family History Library. Read this book first to be better prepared.

NATIONAL AND REGIONAL ARCHIVES

Alaska:
654 West Third Avenue
Anchorage, AK 99501
907-271-2441

Central Plains (Iowa, Kansas, Missouri, Nebraska):
2312 East Bannister Road
Kansas City, MO 64131
816-926-6272

Great Lakes (Illinois, Indiana, Michigan, Minnesota, Ohio, Wisconsin):
7358 South Pulaski Road
Chicago, IL 60629
312-581-7816

Mid-Atlantic (Delaware, Pennsylvania, Maryland, Virginia, West Virginia):
9th & Market Streets

Philadelphia, PA 19107
215-597-3000

New England (Connecticut, Maine, Massachusetts,
New Hawpshire, Rhode Island, Vermont):
380 Trapelo Road
Waltham, MA 02154
617-647-8100

Northeast (New Jersey, New York, Puerto Rico,
Virginia):
201 Varick Street
New York, NY 10014-4811
212-337-1300

Pacific Northwest (Idaho, Oregon, Washington):
6125 Sand Point Way NE
Seattle, WA 98115
206-526-6507

Pacific Sierra (Northern California, Nevada, Hawaii,
Pacific Islands):
1000 Commodore Drive
San Bruno, CA 94066
415-876-9009

Pacific Southwest (Southern California, Arizona):
24000 Avila Road
Laguna Niguel, CA 92677
714-643-4241

Pittsfield (Only microfilm copies)
100 Dan Fox Drive
Pittsfield, MA 01201
413-445-6885

Rocky Mountain (Colorado, Montana, North Dakota,
South Dakota, Utah, Wyoming):
Bldg. 48, Denver Federal Center
Denver, CO 80225-0307
303-236-0817

Southeast (Alabama, Georgia, Florida, Kentucky, Mississippi, North Carolina, South Carolina, Tennessee):
1557 St. Joseph Avenue
East Point, GA 30344
404-763-7477

Southwest (Arkansas, Louisiana, New Mexico, Oklahoma, Texas):
510 West Felix Street
P.O. Box 6216
Ft. Worth, TX 76115
817-334-5525

CENSUS RECORDS

Bureau of the Census
Pittsburg, KS 66762

> Write to obtain information and a list of fees for censuses not yet released to the public (censuses taken since 1920).

Greene, Evarts B., and Harrington, Virginia D. *American Population Before the Federal Census of 1790.* **Baltimore: Genealogical Publishing Co., 1993.**

> Population lists, estimates, and statistics from colonial America and territories such as Illinois Country, Kentucky, and Tennessee. The records were compiled for the purposes of taxation.

Lainhart, Ann S. *State Census Records.* **Baltimore: Genealogical Publishing Co., 1992.**

> This book tells you how to obtain one of the most important genealogical resources, state census records. Lainhart has produced the first comprehensive list of state census records ever published.

Stemmons, John D. *United States Census Compendium.* **Logan, UT: Everton Publishers, 1979.**

> Provides lists of nonfederal censuses. Censuses were also conducted by states and territories.

Thorndale, William, and Dollarhide, William. *Map Guide to the U.S. Federal Censuses: 1790–1920.* **Baltimore: Genealogical Publishing Co., 1991.**

Shows all the U.S. county boundaries from 1790 to 1920 and includes keys on finding census records within a particular locality. Also has an index listing all present-day counties.

PASSENGER LISTS

Colletta, John P. *They Came in Ships.* **Salt Lake City: Ancestry, Inc., 1989, 1993.**

Just over 100 pages in length, this is an easy-to-use beginner's book on the topic.

Immigrant and Passenger Arrivals: A Select Catalog of National Archives Microfilm Publications. **Washington: National Archives Trust Fund Board, 1983, 1991.**

Listing of all the records the Archives has in its collection, detailed reel by reel.

Morton Allan Directory of European Passenger Steamship Arrivals. **Baltimore: Genealogical Publishing Co., 1987.**

Covering 1890 to 1930, this volume lists names of ships arriving according to year, company, and date of arrival at New York, Baltimore, Boston, and Philadelphia.

Newman, John J. *American Naturalization Processes and Procedures, 1790–1985.* **Indianapolis: Indiana Historical Society, 1985.**

Explains how immigration laws work and how they've changed over the years; key information for anyone dealing with the records of the process.

Tepper, Michael. *American Passenger Arrival Records: A Guide to the Records of Immigrants Arriv-*

ing at American Ports by Sail and Steam. **Baltimore: Genealogical Publishing Co., 1993.**

Because the volume of Atlantic ship records is so large and the contents are difficult to use, this book gives a thorough and simple method of accessing and utilizing the information.

ELLIS ISLAND

Ellis Island National Monument
New York, NY 10004
(212) 344-0996

Call or write for information on the monument and museum. Try to plan a visit to this fascinating site.

Fish, Leonard Everett. *Ellis Island: Gateway to the New World*. **New York: Holiday House, 1986.**

A history of immigration through the port of New York, with special focus on the processing at Ellis Island.

Heaps, Willard Allison. *The Story of Ellis Island*. **New York: Seabury Press, 1967.**

Record of the years that Ellis Island served as the immigrants' introduction to the United States, describing the procedures before immigrants were allowed to enter New York.

Jacobs, William Jay. *Ellis Island: New Hope in a New Land*. **New York: Scribner, 1990.**

Traces the history of Ellis Island and immigration to the United States and describes the experiences of immigrants arriving in 1907.

Lawlor, Veronica. *Ellis Island Oral History Project*. **New York: Viking, 1995.**

In their own words, immigrants recall their arrival in the United States. Includes brief biographies and facts about the project, with taped interviews with immigrant Americans. Illustrated.

Levine, Ellen. *If Your Name Was Changed at Ellis Island.* **New York: Scholastic, 1993.**

Describes, in question-and-answer format, the great migration through Ellis Island, from the 1880s to 1914. Features quotes from children and adults who passed through the station.

Stein, R. Conrad. *Ellis Island.* **Chicago: Children's Press, 1992.**

Describes the history, closing, and restoration of the immigration center.

NAMES

Beider, Alexander. *A Dictionary of Jewish Surnames from the Russian Empire.* **Teaneck, NJ: Avotaynu, Inc., 1993.**

The most comprehensive study of Jewish surnames in the Pale of Settlement.

Gorr, Shmuel. *Jewish Personal Names: Their Origin, Derivation, and Diminutive Forms.* **Teaneck, NJ: Avotaynu, Inc., 1992.**

This volume deals with first names, their variations, and origins.

Guggenheimer, Heinrich W., and Guggenheimer, Eva H. *Jewish Family Names and Their Origins: An Etymological Dictionary.* **Hoboken, NJ: Ktav Publishing House, 1992.**

The background and history of Jewish names.

Kolatch, Alfred J. *The New Name Dictionary: Modern English and Hebrew Names.* **New York: Jonathan David, 1989.**

Revision of the author's earlier works, *The Name Diction-ary* and *These Are the Names.*

Singerman, Robert. *Jewish and Hebrew Onomastics: A Bibliography.* **New York and London: Garland, 1977.**

Lists more than 1,000 articles and books on Jewish names and naming.

Smith, Elsdon C. *American Surnames.* **Baltimore: Genealogical Publishing Co., 1969.**

Explores the roots and meanings of different surnames and their many derivatives. Covers almost all ethnic, religious, and geographical names, including Jewish names.

Chapter 10
Research on the Holocaust and Your Ancestors' Roots

If your search for family takes you to the Holocaust, you will be touching on the greatest disaster ever to befall the Jewish people, but also one that happened in the age of communications. That has made it one of the best recorded disasters in history, covered by books, articles, film, and other media. Unfortunately, however, there are few indexes to help locate given individuals among the millions killed or lost. Those that do exist are often not in English.

Two great centers of information have been built. Yad Vashem is Israel's Holocaust museum and memorial. It includes a library and an area called the Hall of Names, with more than 100,000 books, and 3 million "Pages of Testimony" written by the relatives of Holocaust victims. These writings include the names of parents, spouses, and children, and birth and death dates and places. The writers also include how they were related to the victims.

The other great center is the United States Holocaust Memorial Museum, which includes the world's second-largest collection of eyewitness accounts and thousands of photographs and keepsakes of the victims.

Yizkor Books
One way to study the lives of lost relatives is through Yizkor books, writings about Jewish communities that existed before the war. The writers remember the towns and town life, and list townspeople and what happened to them.

Yad Vashem houses some 800 Yizkor books. Other large collections are at the Library of Congress in Washington, the New York Public Library in Manhattan, and the University of California in Los Angeles. Canadian genealogists can find a collection at the Jewish Public Library of Montreal.

A number of organizations have been formed to trace missing persons. These organizations are still active and can be helpful in locating information. They are listed in the **Resources**.

The International Tracing Service, a branch of the International Red Cross, has collected more than 40 million index cards on persons involved in the Holocaust. The Yad Vashem Holocaust memorial also has these records and will respond more quickly than the Red Cross to questions about them.

An American counterpart, the Holocaust and War Victims Tracing and Information Center, is part of the American Red Cross, and will forward search requests to the International Tracing Service.

Finding Your Ancestral Village

Earlier we discussed interviewing members of your family and using vital records to begin the process of tracking your history back to its origins. We explored finding the gateway city through which your forebears entered the United States, and then tracing back further to the means of transport that got them to that city.

Now let's take the next practical step that can be done with normal resources—locating the city or town your relatives hailed from. It's an exciting step. No longer will your family simply come from Russia or Poland, but from Zhitomir or Lodz.

Once you know the name of the town, a rich vein of historical information may open. There may be photos of the streets your ancestors walked, the square where they shopped, or the school they attended. A city or town book or a Yizkor book may exist. There may be old newspapers, and someday, you might plan a visit to the area. There may, in fact, still be members of your family living there.

Marriage records can provide valuable information on your ancestors. This undated photo depicts a traditional Jewish wedding.

Even if you never make the trip, however, your search for family background can now continue. As is done in the United States, vital records are kept at European local government offices. You can start with the relatives who came to the United States, and work backward to the generation before them.

Review Your Personal Information

During your interviews with relatives, you asked what town the family came from. Review that information now. Look for consistent answers from two or more persons. Also look again at physical items for any markings; the town name may be on a photo or other object.

One word of warning. It's common for people to say they came from Moscow or Hamburg when what they really mean is a smaller community near these major cities. Ask your relatives to be as specific as possible.

Check Vital Records

The name of the town your ancestors came from may be on birth, marriage, or death certificates. Look also at passports and citizenship papers. You may have ordered a copy of your relative's Social Security application. This may also contain a birthplace.

Depending on the date, passenger arrival lists may specify "Last residence" or place of birth.

Did your relative belong to a *Landsmannschaften*, an organization of former residents of a town or region? These organizations often purchased group burial plots. The name of the town will likely be on the cemetery records.

If your relative was a male born between 1886 and 1897, he would have been required to register for the World War I draft, and his draft card would give an exact place of birth. If he served, this information is available through the National Archives collection of military records, or through the LDS Family History Centers. Internet users can receive a copy of a World War I draft file by sending an e-mail message to wwidraft@cgsg.com.

If your relative traveled out of the United States, he or she would have put an exact birthplace on the application for a passport. Applications made before 1925 are kept by the National Archives and at Family History Centers.

Noncitizens had to file for Alien Registration if they resided in the United States after 1941. This application would record the applicant's birthplace. You can get a copy of this document under the Freedom of Information Act.

Resources

HOLOCAUST RECORDS

Gedenkbuch. **Koblenz, Germany, 1986.**

Lists 128,000 West German Jews who perished in the Holocaust, with birthdate, place deported from, and place deported to.

HIAS (Hebrew Immigrant Aid Society)
333 Seventh Avenue
New York, NY 10001

Group formed to assisted Holocaust families in the 1940s and 1950s. They maintain case files of some 70,000 cases and will do a search for a twenty-five dollar fee.

Holocaust and War Victims Tracing and Information Center
Central Maryland Chapter
4700 Mount Hope Drive
Baltimore, MD 21215-3200
800-848-9277

This organization may be useful if you believe that any of your relatives may have died during the Holocaust.

International Tracing Service (ITS)
Grosse Allee 5-9
34454 Arolsen, Germany

Memorial to the Jews Deported from France, 1942–1944: Documentation of the Deportation of the Victims of the Final Solution in France. **New York: Klarsfeld Foundation, 1983.**

Lists 70,000 Jews deported from France to concentration camps, with birth date and place.

Mokotoff, Gary, and Amdur-Sack, Sallyann. *Where Once We Walked: A Guide to the Jewish Communities Destroyed in the Holocaust.* **Teaneck, NJ: Avotaynu Press, 1991.**

More than 21,000 towns in central and eastern Europe are detailed.

Search Bureau for Missing Relatives
P.O. Box 92
Jerusalem 91000, Israel
02-612471, 02-612472

U.S. Holocaust Memorial Museum
100 Raoul Wallenberg Place SW
Washington, DC 20024-2150
202-488-0400

If you live near Washington, DC, or plan a visit there, this important museum is not to be missed. Its powerful exhibits and interactive programs serve to educate the public about one of humankind's greatest tragedies.

If you are on the Internet, you can get information about the museum at World Wide Web site http://www.ushmm.org.

FINDING ANCESTORS' BIRTHPLACES

Immigration and Naturalization Service
Freedom of Information
Room 5304, 425 I Street NW
Washington, DC 20536
202-514-1554

This office can provide copies of Alien Registration.

U.S. State Department
Passport Office
Bureau of Consular Affairs, FAIM/RS, Room 1239
22d and C Streets NW
Washington, DC 20520

Contact this office for passport applications after 1925.

Conclusion

Putting It All Together

If you recall, one of the key ground rules of genealogy is to share your findings with others—other genealogists, and especially the members of the family you've just researched. The best way to do that is by publishing your work.

Let's make it clear that our use of the term publishing has nothing to do with multimillion-dollar printing plants, national author tours, and such. It may not even have to do with books. (Some of the best publishing these days is being done in video and other electronic forms.) Publishing simply means putting your work and thoughts together in a way that others can access and understand. This will be important when future generations want to research their ancestors. They will be able to refer to your work. Following are some ways to present your findings in an interesting and creative manner.

Scrapbook

If your work is already in some kind of book form, it can easily be turned into a scrapbook by writing some descriptive pages about the materials in the book and inserting them in appropriate places between the materials. You might choose to organize the materials in generation order, starting with what you've learned and accumulated about your parents first, then your grandparents, and so on back. Insert photos, maps, transport tickets, old newspaper articles, and other items, along with the material they relate to. There's no reason to confine your materials to family matters. Some of the best scrapbooks also contain "atmospheric" materials. For example, a section about your family in the 1950s might include an "I Like Ike" campaign button or a Howdy Doody TV show toy wrapping. Photos of items may be inserted if the items themselves are too large.

Audio-Video Presentation

If you've ever seen a well-done documentary on TV, you know how much sound and motion can add to history. Adding audio to your scrapbook is easy. Just record a description of each page or section on a cassette tape and insert it in the inside cover of the book. Be sure to ring a bell or use some other sound to indicate time to turn the page.

Video is more ambitious, but also much more involving. Lay out your history as a series of exhibits to shoot with the family camcorder. Pan (move left to right) slowly over each exhibit as you describe it. A written script or well thought out notes will help enormously. It's tough to do the camera work and think up the words at the same time. It is all right to video still photos of people or places; they'll come out fine and look like part of the movie. Just start the camera with them already in view and keep the camera on them during the description. You can even try panning a little. With a picture of a person, start with the feet and move up to finish on the face. But always move the camera slowly and watch for any glare of lights on glossy surfaces.

As you may know, documentary producers commonly cut to interviews or parts of interviews between depictions. You can too, if you have the equipment and know how to edit. But even if you don't, do include interviews. There's nothing as interesting as people who were there, telling their life stories in their own words.

When your presentation is ready, don't be shy about promoting it. Make it a family gathering. Offer to make copies for family members who can't be there. And don't forget to take a bow. You've earned it!

Newsletter

You don't need to finish your genealogical study to begin to present your findings. Many researchers create a periodic newsletter and mail it (or e-mail it) to all concerned. You could do this monthly, though two to four times yearly might be enough. Talk about what you've learned—and also the questions that have come up. They might be the spark to someone's remembering the answers you seek.

Writing a Family History

At some point in your research, you will probably feel ready to compile your results in writing. This may be well before your family research is "finished"—remember, family history is a potentially endless project, so you should never feel inadequate for stopping before the end. You may simply reach a point where you cannot research any further, because of time constraints or because of a gap in records. But a stumbling block does not have to mean that your work is finished. Writing a family history gives you the opportunity to lay out all you have done in a manner that can be read and enjoyed by family members and future generations. Once you start writing, you will probably find that you have uncovered much more information than you thought you had.

If you have designed a family tree, you might make this the cover of your written family history. Adding photos as well as names of ancestors to your family tree is a particularly nice touch.

Decide on a focus for your family history. Will you focus on a particular ancestor, sketching a portrait of him or her and then going on to trace his or her descendants? Will you focus on a particular ancestral line? You may decide to tell the story of your project: where you began, how you found out what you know, whom you spoke with.

One way to make your story particularly fascinating is to put it in historical context. Provide a historical backdrop—mention, for example, who was the political leader at the time a particular ancestor was born, or if a war occurred in his or her lifetime.

Most important, you will need to back up what you write by stating where you found the information. You might even include photocopies of documents such as birth certificates or military service records; they serve as proof as well as adding interest to your work. Include copies of pedigree charts and family group sheets so your relatives can see their roles in the larger family context.

Family Reunion

Presenting the results of your research at a family reunion can be fun and rewarding. Here is your chance to gather together the people who will find your work most meaningful. It is also your opportunity to thank those who helped you with your research and show them what they have contributed to.

The first thing you will probably want to do at a reunion is pass out copies of a written family history. If your family is very large and this would require a huge number of photocopies, another option is to put your family history in an album where the pages are covered in plastic. You might insert photos or copies of documents as illustrations. Put the album on a table where family members will readily see it—on the table with the guest book, for example. This way, interested family members will be able to leaf through your family history without damage to the pages, and you will have saved yourself the expense of photocopying.

If you have compiled an audio or video presentation, you might make this the centerpiece of your event. This can also be a way to interest younger children who might otherwise find family history an unexciting topic.

Don't worry if you were unable to put together an audio or visual presentation; your research can still be presented in a way that will appeal to family members. Be creative. Mount a large map on cardboard, showing with brightly colored push pins where your ancestors came from and where they settled in the United States. Draw a time line of historical events and make your way through history, explaining where your family was during specific historical periods and how they were affected by world events. Ask relatives to bring photos; put them up on a bulletin board or

have relatives pass them around and explain their signifi-
cance. Draw a large version of your family tree on construction paper and mount it on a wall. Have family members
sign their names or paste their pictures next to their names
on the family tree.

If your family is not in the habit of holding reunions,
don't be discouraged. With some help from parents, grandparents, or siblings, you can organize one yourself. Reunions
are usually held during the summer, when adults and children are more likely to be on vacation and when gatherings
can involve outdoor activities.

Even with a small family, a family reunion is an ambitious
undertaking. Your task will be easier if you work with other
family members who are interested in helping to plan the
reunion. Together, gather phone numbers and addresses of
family members. Make a form letter describing the reunion
and the time and place it will be held. The location might be
a town or city where your ancestors settled, where many of
your relatives have lived, or where many family members are
buried. Make sure that the reunion site is convenient for a
majority of family members. A visit to family homes or
cemeteries can be one of the planned reunion events. You
might advertise the event in genealogical magazines, local
newspapers, or genealogical society publications. This may
attract family members who live far away or who have lost
touch with relatives.

Ask your parents or grandparents if there are any family
recipes that can be prepared for the reunion. A meal featur-
ing Aunt Melanie's famous latkes (potato pancakes) is not
only tasty—it is also a way to celebrate your heritage and the
bond of family. Storytelling, songs, even a Yiddish lesson led
by your great-grandmother can be enjoyed by family members of all ages.

Your family reunion may lead to discussion about forming
a family association, if one has not already been organized
for your family. A family association can be formed for one
surname line, and may be named after the immigrant ancestor ("The Descendants of Solomon Abramowitz," for exam-

ple). As the organizer of your family association, you can collect family group sheets from members and perhaps even send out a newsletter with updates on your genealogical research.

Whatever medium you choose, communicate your work. The whole idea of a family is for members to be concerned with and help other members. And there's nothing better to communicate about than the history that unites you all.

Resources

COMPILING A FAMILY HISTORY

Barnes, Donald R., and Lackey, Richard S. *Write It Right: A Manual for Writing Family Histories and Genealogies.* **Rockville, MD: Lyon Press, 1983.**

> If you are having trouble getting started writing your family history, check this book for tips on how to organize and present your research.

Cheney, Theodore A. Rees. *Writing Creative Nonfiction: How to Use Fiction Techniques to Make Your Nonfiction More Interesting, Dramatic and Vivid.* **Cincinnati, OH: Writer's Digest Books, 1987.**

> Your family history is probably a fascinating story; why not do it justice by writing it in the most interesting way possible? This book can give you assistance in doing just that.

Fletcher, William P. *Record Your Family History.* **Berkeley, CA: Ten Speed Press, 1989.**

> Consult this source if you seek to make an audio or visual presentation of your family history.

Lackey, Richard S. *Cite Your Sources: A Manual for Documenting Family Histories and Genealogical Records.* **Jackson: University Press of Mississippi, 1985.**

> Citing sources correctly is crucial to writing a family history that will stand the test of time. This book will help you to ensure that your work can be proved accurate. It provides instructions on how to cite sources such as birth certificates and gravestones.

McLaughlin, Paul. *A Family Remembers*. **North Vancouver, BC: Self-Counsel Press, 1993.**

An up-to-date guide to creating a family memoir with video cameras and tape recorders.

Zinsser, William. *On Writing Well: An Informal Guide to Writing Nonfiction*, **3d ed. New York: Harper and Row, 1985.**

The facts alone do not guarantee that your family history will be interesting and readable. This book provides guidelines on writing a nonfiction piece.

Glossary

apprenticeship Practice of learning a trade by on-the-job experience under a skilled worker.

borscht Soup of Russian origin made of beets and served hot or cold, sometimes with sour cream.

diaspora The breaking up and scattering of a people.

gefilte fish Minced fish formed into balls or cakes and cooked in fish stock or tomato sauce.

get The Jewish document of divorce.

Inquisition Former Roman Catholic tribunal that tried and condemned people for heresy.

Ivriim An ancient people thought to be the ancestors of the Jews.

Kabbalah Secret writings about superstition and the forces of good and evil.

ketubah The Jewish document of marriage.

Landsmannschaften Groups of people from the same town or region who commonly buy burial plots together.

mitzvoth Performance of good deeds for others.

monotheism Belief that there is only one God.

naturalization Process of being admitted to citizenship of a country.

pharaoh One of a series of rulers of ancient Egypt.

pogrom Organized massacre of helpless people.

polygamy Marriage in which a spouse may have more than one mate at a time.

rabbi The leader of a Jewish congregation.

shtetl A small community of Jews.

Talmud Series of writings that explain the Torah.

Torah The books of the Old Testament written by the ancient Hebrews, including the Talmud.

yarmulke   Skullcap worn by males in Orthodox and Conservative Judaism.

Yiddish   Language invented by European Jews in the 1300s.

Index

ABOUT THE AUTHOR

The son of Jewish immigrants, **Jay Schleifer** grew up in New York City. He is a publishing company executive and freelance writer. He has taught public school and served as the editor of the national classroom publication, *Know Your World Extra*. He and his wife live in the Midwest.

ILLUSTRATION CREDITS

Cover, © Kim Sonsky; cover inset, courtesy of the Sonsky family. Pp. 2, 4, 6, 19, 32, 35, 43, 45, 48, 68, 69, 70, 81, 92, 115, 121, 122, 135, 149, BETTMANN. *Color insert*: p. 2, © Michael J. Howell/International Stock; pp. 3, 5, 13, 15, 16, BETTMANN; p. 4, © Deborah Gilbert/The Image Bank; p. 6, © Stephen Marks/ The Image Bank; p. 7, © Chuck Fishman/The Image Bank; p. 8, 12, © Stacy Rosenstock/Impact Visuals; p. 9, 14, © AP/Wide World Photos; p. 10, © Tom McKitterick/Impact Visuals; p. 11, © Lindsay Silverman/International Stock.

LAYOUT AND DESIGN

Kim Sonsky